MOUNT MITCHELL
Its Railroad and Toll Road

Jeff Lovelace

Cover Design by David Dixon

The Overmountain Press

JOHNSON CITY, TENNESSEE

ISBN 0-932807-84-4

1 2 3 4 5 6 7 8 9 0

This book is dedicated to the men who built and worked on the Mount Mitchell Railroad Line.

Acknowledgments

I wish to acknowledge with gratitude the persons, firms, or institutions who generously provided assistance in the search for illustrative material or background information utilized in compiling **Mount Mitchell: Its Railroad and Toll Road**.

Mrs. Mary Charlotte McCall, Decatur, Ga., the finest teacher I have ever known. Her kindness is unmatched; her spirit is peerless. *(Thank you for believing in me. Your faith taught me how to believe in myself.)* Steven Blahut, Morganton, N.C.; my dear mother, who rescued me when I used poor grammar; Mrs. Marion P. Casstevens, Black Mountain, N.C.; Robert P. Crockett, Williamsport, Penna.; Walter C. Casler, Corry, Penna.; Mrs. Mary Lane at the Historical Foundation of the Presbyterian and Reformed Churches, Montreat, N.C.; David Biddix and brother, Donald Biddix, of Ridgecrest and Black Mountain, N.C.; Kent Schwarzkopf, Gettysburg, Penna.; Retired District Ranger Jim Haynes, former district manager for the Department of the Interior (Blue Ridge Parkway) Swannanoa District; Allan Paul, Raleigh, N.C.; the Rev. Gorman Burgin, Black Mountain, N.C.; Eric Rudolph, Chattanooga, Tenn.; Wendell Begley, Black Mountain, N.C.; Robert Conway, (retired) from N.C. Dept. of Archives and History, Weaverville, N.C.; Samuel Foreman, Madison, Tenn.; Dr. George Deike, Cass, W.V.; Michael Oneal, Tullahoma, Tenn.; Arthur J. Hemphill, Jr., Black Mountain, N.C.; and thanks to the members of the Reference Staff at Pack Memorial Library—Laura Gaskin, Chuck Cady, and Lewis Buck.

Photo Credits

American Forestry, Vol. XXI, February, 1915 by Raymond Pullman

Barnhill Collection, Pack Memorial Library, Asheville, North Carolina

David Biddix, Ridgecrest, North Carolina

Rev. Gorman Burgin, Black Mountain, North Carolina

Mrs. Marion Perley Casstevens, Black Mountain, North Carolina

Robert P. Crockett, Williamsport, Pennsylvania

Arthur J. Hemphill, Black Mountain, North Carolina

Norfolk-Southern Corporation Archives, Atlanta, Georgia

Presbyterian Church (U.S.A.) Department of History, Montreat, North Carolina

Contents

Introduction

To one who loves railroads and railroading, the story of the development of the Mount Mitchell Railroad is a captivating chapter of the mountain's history. An enormous challenge to reach Eastern America's highest peak by a narrow-gauge railroad was achieved by Dickey & Campbell and Perley & Crockett. The historical significance was an important factor in the composition of this book. This is an historical overview; every effort was made to see that it remains as accurate and true as humanly possible.

My first obstruction in the research of this publication was the fact that there were no remaining survivors who worked on the Mount Mitchell Railroad. My second obstacle was that very few authors have documented this fascinating story. I spent several weeks indexing and retrieving information from the old *Asheville Citizen* newspaper at the Pack Memorial Library. My research carried me through the entire western portion of North Carolina, in an effort that went on for six years.

Since most of the roadbed is now densely overgrown, my third barrier was to locate an accurate map of the route from Black Mountain to near Mount Mitchell. The difficulty was twofold: First, the roadbed was overgrown and the crossties and trestles were long gone; Second, the railroad did deviate from the Toll Road at Long Gap, which is explained in this book.

In compiling the text and illustration material, new and existing information were both carefully blended in with many never-before published photographs and interviews. I made my best attempt to capture an in-depth study of the construction and operation of this most interesting local railroad and toll road in Western North Carolina; but many bits and pieces are still uncovered because the preservation of knowledge and historical documents was seldom to be found. I hope you will find this story to be as enjoyable as I have.

Chronology—The Mount Mitchell Railroad/Toll Road

Nov. 24, 1910—Preliminary steps taken to map out road to Mount Mitchell

Nov. 2, 1911—Preliminary survey done for mountain road

Nov. 3, 1911—Dickey and Campbell filed deeds for land in Black Mountain

Nov. 14, 1911—Construction authorized by Montreat Managing Committee

Dec. 12, 1911—Construction started at Black Mountain, N.C.

Dec. 14, 1911—Dickey, Campbell and Co. granted right-of-way for logging railroad

Mar. 6, 1912—Agreement made with Mountain Retreat Assoc. to construct railroad

Mar. 29, 1912—Mountain railroad now near completion—6 miles now graded

May 4, 1912—W.H. Belk sold right-of-way to Dickey, Campbell and Co.

June 21, 1912—Sawmill is just about completed

Dec. 13, 1912—The first logs were loaded

Dec. 26, 1912—Dickey and Campbell form a corporation in North Carolina

Feb. 10, 1913—Dickey and Campbell bought an "American" log loader

June 1, 1913—18 miles of track laid to a point near foot of Mount Mitchell

July 22, 1913—Governor Craig christens railroad, opening day

Aug. 1, 1913—Dickey and Campbell leased Climax No. 5 SN 1235, Class B, 42 ton

Sept. 27, 1913—Dickey and Campbell sells out to Perley and Crockett

Oct. 8, 1913—One of largest lumber deals in state history, D&C to P&C

Apr. 13, 1914—Southern Railway leased D&C rails and fastenings to extend railroad

June 25, 1914—Trail to the inn at the summit was cleared

July 8, 1914—Fire destroys $10,000 worth of timber near the summit

Aug. 20, 1914—Moving pictures made at the top of the mountain

Jan. 1, 1915—Mount Mitchell monument found destroyed

Jan. 12, 1915—Sen. Weaver introduced a bill for the creation of the Mitchell Park Comm.

Jan. 13, 1915—Governor Craig's speech to the American Forestry Association

Feb. 16, 1915—Southern Railway leased five more miles of rails to D&C

Feb. 22, 1915—Senate passed Weaver Bill to appropriate $20,000 for the park

Mar. 3, 1915—Governor Craig pushed through a bill to make the state park

Mar. 31, 1915—Governor Craig announced special committee for purchasing Mount Mitchell

May 20, 1915—Mount Mitchell Monument was not dynamited as had been stated earlier

July 14, 1915—Governor Craig makes a visit to Mount Mitchell

July 16, 1915—Railroad formally and officially opened to passenger traffic

July 17, 1915—Governor Craig names a commission to erect a monument

Aug. 3, 1915—Opening of the Mount Mitchell Station at Southern Railway

Aug. 9, 1915—Several new passenger cars were built for Railway Co.

Sept. 24, 1915—Plans to build a hotel on Point Lookout

Nov. 13, 1915—State finalized deal to buy Mount Mitchell at $5.00 an acre

Dec. 4, 1915—Southern Railway leases 2½ more miles of rail to D&C

Apr. 4, 1916—Ten new cars built for the Mount Mitchell Railroad Line

Apr. 5, 1916—Wooden observation tower being built by Perley and Crockett

May 27, 1916—Camp Alice is completed, dining hall and tents constructed

June 12, 1916—More moving pictures taken on route to the summit

July 31, 1917—State Corporation Commission claims P&C are charging more than 2½¢ a mile.

Nov. 11, 1917—Old fine surfaces for P&C cutting trees beyond the boundary of the watershed

July 22, 1918—Mount Mitchell Railroad makes new record for amount of persons transported

Aug. 4, 1918—People use automobiles to catch the Mount Mitchell train

Aug. 22, 1918—Mount Mitchell Railroad suspends trips because of World War I

Sept. 26, 1918—Mount Mitchell road to be improved

Oct. 3, 1918—Lula Howie sues railroad for injuries sustained on excursion trip

June 24, 1919—Passenger service halted, railroad requires entire use

Aug. 9, 1921—Passenger service again considered

Aug. 15, 1921—Logging operations completed, no more timber cut

Aug. 26, 1921—Airplane landing on Mount Mitchell is sought by Turner

Aug. 31, 1921—Incorporation of Mount Mitchell Development Co. capital stock is divided

Sept. 15, 1921—Condemnation action taken against Montreat for right-of-way

Sept. 22, 1921—Proposed turnpike discussed with Asheville Board of Trade

Sept. 24, 1921—Both sides heard in argument over proposed turnpike

Oct. 10, 1921—Mount Mitchell Development Co. restrained from building the road

Oct. 21, 1921—Hearing began on highway injunction

Nov. 13, 1921—Survey head cites Mount Mitchell route

Dec. 10, 1921—Mount Mitchell road case completed—Supreme Court decision soon

Jan. 1, 1922—Rushing work on scenic highway, one mile already paved in cinders

Apr. 9, 1922—Will change road course, will go around Montreat watershed for six miles

May 29, 1922—Work proceeding rapidly on the Mount Mitchell toll road

June 26, 1922—Official toll road dedication and opening

1926—Old Mount Mitchell stone tower completed, took two years to build

Sept. 1928—Cannonball Baker sets world record driving up Mount Mitchell

May 1936—Highway Commission and Public Works take over the toll road

1939—Section of Parkway between North Carolina #80 and Black Mountain Gap was finished

June 4, 1959—Old Mount Mitchell stone observation tower was torn down

The Dickey and Campbell Days: Starting the Railroad

Even before 1910, residents and businessmen from Black Mountain, North Carolina, were very interested in building a toll road or railroad from Black Mountain to Mount Mitchell. The residents clearly desired a more direct route to the infamous mountain for tourism. Railroad tycoons, however, wanted to get their hands on the enormous virgin forests in the Black Mountain range. The businessmen saw the forest for its resources, and the townspeople wanted Mount Mitchell for sightseeing, fishing, hunting, and picnicking, and to take walks among the clouds.

It was on November 24, 1910, that several Black Mountain residents made an inspection trip of the proposed railroad/motor toll road route, accompanied by an expert engineer. Walking the mountains for about three days, they got an estimate of the cost of the road and saw what obstacles stood in its way. They believed that by crossing the ridges and the high peaks, a feasible gradient could be built. A bond referendum was to be passed, and it was stated that the projected toll road could be built for less than $100,000. The township of Black Mountain hoped to collect enough toll fares to pay for the construction of the road and still have enough left over to start a sinking fund for retiring the road bonds.

Then in 1911, the partnership of C.A. Dickey and J.C. Campbell began to formulate their plans to build a logging railroad which would extend from just east of the town of Black Mountain to a point near the foot of Mount Mitchell. To gain access to much of the proposed railroad property, several right-of-ways had to be obtained. After Dickey and Campbell purchased the timber lines, a preliminary survey was done by John N. Shoolirell and H. Roths, both from Waynesville, N.C.

They spent several weeks in the mountains, inspecting until November 1911. They concluded that the railroad would consist of several switchbacks and would not exceed a grade of five percent. This gradient would be safe for any passengers riding on the proposed line. Dickey and Campbell had intended to build a narrow gauge railroad, but they realized that the standard gauge would enable passengers on the tourist trains to transfer without changing cars, a gain in convenience.

Surveyed by C.A. Dodds, Civil Engineer, a proposed rail line ran along the property of the Mountain Retreat Association for about six miles. According to the Buncombe County Deed Book, after the Managing Committee held a meeting on December 14, 1911, "the Mountain Retreat Association granted to Dickey and Campbell a right-of-way, easement, and privilege to grade, construct, and lay down crossties, rails, and other structure necessary to run and operate a railroad over the lands of the Mountain Retreat Association." Dickey and Campbell would pay $500 per mile to the Mountain Retreat Association for the entire length of the railroad. The right-of-way was to be 40 feet in width, and they were to cut down only enough timber necessary to build the railroad. This easement included a payment of 15 cents for every crosstie that Dickey and Campbell installed. The Association reserved the right to all wood and timber on the said right-of-way. After negotiating, the Mountain Retreat Association sold the right-of-way for $3,030.35.

By March 29, 1912, six miles of the roadbed were graded, and the rail gang was ready to lay down rails at once. A hundred men were employed in the work, grading 125,000 square feet a day.

The sawmill was going up fast, with the basement floor already finished. The prospect of profits from tourism proved to be a magnet for proposals. J.M. Chiles and a Mr. Smith from Buncombe County wanted to lease the road after its construction in order to take tourists up the mountain on Thomas A. Edison's storage-battery electric cars. The cabin at Mitchell's Peak would be enlarged and a park built at Hemphill Springs. There were even plans to sell lots to those connected with operating the line, to build summer cottages.

Another right-of-way was sold to Dickey and Campbell on May 4, 1912, by W.H. Belk of Mecklenburg County. For the sum of $170, Dickey and Campbell received the right to construct their railroad from a point on the Southern Railway, to a gap in the mountain, on the dividing line between Buncombe and McDowell Counties. An easement was also granted for 40 feet in width, located and staked out over the land of W.H. Belk in Black Mountain. Originally, Dickey and Campbell acquired the timber rights to 9,000 acres of land on the southern and eastern flanks of the Black Mountains.

Things moved rapidly, and the first logs were loaded on December

13, 1912, only 364 days after construction of the road was started at Black Mountain.

At nearly the same time, in 1908, the Murchison Boundary in Yancey County was surveyed for timber lines. This survey included over 11,000 acres at the upper end of the Cane Creek Valley. However, because of rolling ground, 30 percent was added to the acreage, making the tract over 13,000 acres.

Nearby, another railroad was constructed, which joined the Dickey and Campbell line just below Stepps Gap. The Brown Brothers Lumber Company's ownership was brief, only about a year, but much of their spruce timber was purchased by Perley and Crockett (the successors to Dickey and Campbell), who transported the logs over their own railroad line.

C.A. Dickey and J.C. Campbell joined on December 26, 1912, to form a corporation in North Carolina, after dissolving their corporation in Smythe County, Virginia. They paid $600,000 into the new corporation, $300,000 from each partner.

In order to get the logs on their logging trucks, Dickey, Campbell and Company needed a log loader, and on February 10, 1913, they purchased one "American" log loader (serial #626) from American Hoist and Derrick Company. Dickey, Campbell and Company agreed to pay, besides freight charges, the sum of $6,000 as follows: $1,000 cash on receipt of the Bill of Lading, and the balance in five equal payments of $1,000 each, maturing at sixty-day intervals from the date of the shipment. Deferred payments were to be covered by six percent interest-bearing notes.

Pessimists had predicted that it would take ten years, from start of construction, to haul the lumber to the mill. But several hundred men were put to work, and after only two years of hard labor and over 700 tons of dynamite, the road was completed to a point near the foot of Mount Mitchell, a wonderful achievement of modern engineering.

The official opening day was July 22, 1913, for the Mount Mitchell Railroad, a significant event for North Carolina. With a poetic eloquence tinged with Biblical echoes, the *Asheville Citizen* reported that Governor Locke Craig said:

"This is not the first time I have stood upon this historic spot. I have hunted the black bear through all these forests and have seen the Toe River when the stream was filled with ice and the hills were clad in mantles of snow.... This is the beginning of magnificent things. This railway is a pioneer, as was the first white man looking down from this gap upon a wilderness filled with savage beasts and still more savage men and saw a country to be subdued. So from here we look down upon a mighty waste that shall be converted into the most beautiful park in all the world. It would be appropriate to read the first chapter of Genesis where it says, "God shall let the waters under the heaven be gathered together under one place and let the dry land appear and it was so." Geologists tell us that this was the first dry land on the globe. Here is where God began."

But for operation, locomotives and rolling stock were necessary. An agreement was made on August 1, 1913, between the Climax Manufacturing Company and Dickey, Campbell and Company, Inc., in Black Mountain, N.C. The railway company leased one 42-ton Class B locomotive, a 36-inch gauge duplicate of locomotive No. 4, for $6,000. It was lettered "Dickey and Campbell No. 5, Shop No. 1235." The rolling stock rental was payable by the lessor to the lessee, as follows: Terms $1,500 cash, $1,500 in six months with interest at six percent, $1,500 dollars in nine months with interest at 6 percent, $1,500 dollars in twelve months also with interest at 6 percent.

The Southern Railway Company leased on April 13, 1914, to Dickey and Campbell enough rails and fastenings to lay and construct a logging railroad. It was to extend from a point on the line of railroad of the Railway Company about one mile east of Black Mountain, in a northerly direction, partly through Buncombe, McDowell, and Yancey Counties in North Carolina. The distance was 15 miles and 3,400 feet, more or less.

Arrangements were also made on April 13, 1914; February 16, 1915; and December 4, 1915, with Dickey, Campbell and Company by Southern Railway to lease enough rails and fastenings to run their railroad track to an extent of approximately 23 miles and 760 feet. This agreement was made so the railroad line could expand from a point of the Southern Railway (about one mile east of Black Mountain) into a northerly direction, partly through the Counties of Buncombe and McDowell, and into Yancey County. The breakdown of leased material is as follows:

April 13, 1914
163,847 feet of 50 lb. rails . . . . 1219 tons, 224 lbs.

8,176 angle bars . . . . .46 tons, 1611 lbs.
Track bolts . . . . .1 ton, 147 lbs.
                                     Total: 1,266 tons, 1982 lbs.
February 16, 1915
52,800 feet of 50 lb. rails . . . . .392 tons, 1920 lbs.
3,000 angle bars . . . . .17 tons, 920 lbs.
                                     Total: 410 tons, 600 lbs.
December 4, 1915
26,837 feet of 50 lb. rails . . . . .199 tons, 1523 lbs.
1,513 angle bars . . . . .8 tons, 1749 lbs.
                                     Total: 208 tons, 1032 lbs.

The total value of all material combined was $94,280.65. The rental of all material leased was to be $5,656.84 per year, and it was to be paid in monthly installments of $471.40. This was to be paid for two years, until released.

Because of the steepness of the terrain, the general public was apparently astonished by the plan to build a narrow gauge railroad to the upper slopes of the range. The railroad was, however, built using mules, dynamite, and a great deal of hard labor.

Much of the lumber that was obtained at Mount Mitchell was clear spruce. This particular kind of wood was very much in demand for use in manufacturing airplanes in 1914 because of its density and light weight. Most of the wood used in making airplanes was shipped to England. Although the railroad line was built to gain access to the timber in the Black Mountains, the owners of the line, thinking of tourism, debated as early as 1913 about using the railroad for transporting exclusive parties of passengers.

A question of vital importance to "railroaders" and, of course, to model railroaders who enthusiastically like to model nostalgic, historical railroads like this is whether it was narrow gauge or standard gauge. Showing a picturesque ingenuity, the answer is—it was both. Original plans were to build a standard gauge railroad line, but it was changed to become a narrow gauge, 3-foot line. However, a third rail was added at the sawmill and the interchange so that the railroad could run both standard and narrow gauge stock. (This is called dual-gauge track.) Also, there was an idea of using Edison's storage-battery electric cars on the line after it was built, but there seems to be no evidence that this was ever realized.

The Route of the Railroad: Pathway of Progress

The route of the Mount Mitchell Railroad first passed through Montreat, the Presbyterian Assembly's summer home, then wound up the side of a ridge from Sourwood Gap to a knoll on a ridge above Long Gap, a climb of 740 feet. The grade then crossed back to the far side of the ridge and skirted Graybeard Mountain (once spelled "Greybeard") and Pinnacle on a climb to Camp Alice and Stepps Gap (once spelled "Steps Gap"), where loggers were busy cutting the spruce pine of Mount Mitchell's slopes.

Overall, the railroad climbed 3,500 feet over a distance of about 21 miles. For the Mount Mitchell Railroad to be able to ascend 3,500 feet, with only three trestles and nine switchbacks, and still maintain a gradient of five and one-half percent, was an amazing feat, then and now.

Construction of the railroad, and its timely completion, was also surprising when compared with other roads. For example, just a year after work began in 1911, the first trainload of logs was hauled out of the mountains over the continually extending railroad. By June of 1913, eighteen miles of track had been laid, and the railroad reached the slopes of Clingmans Peak. By 1914, it reached the 5,800-foot contour, approximately eight tenths of a mile below the summit of Mount Mitchell.

The railroad was curvaceous, no doubt of it: the curves on the Mount Mitchell Railroad varied from 10 to 55 percent, with one of them being as abrupt as **96 degrees**.

Camp Alice was the terminus of the railroad for passengers. From there the Perley and Crockett Logging Railroad followed the eastern flank of the range to Potato Hill (once spelled Potatoe Hill), and westward across Stepps Gap toward Balsam Gap. Since spruce and balsam were the primary targets of the logging operations, much of the railroad track was built along the 5,800-foot contour near the lower limit of the spruce-fir forest.

Aerial photography of the roadbed shows that much of the road can still be seen. However, certain sections have deteriorated severely. The Pot Cove Gap area and around Little and Big Slaty are probably the worst. Rocks have fallen into the road, and sometimes part of the road is washed out; but most of the time it's simply overgrown with trees, vines, briars, and thickets. While the trees have kept the grades from eroding, they make the roadbed almost unrecognizable.

Camp Alice was a series of log structures with roofs anchored to the rocks of the mountainside to prevent them from blowing away in high wintry winds. The largest building served as a kitchen and dining hall for the loggers, while smaller cabins provided sleeping accommodations. The large dining hall and sleeping rooms, with tents fully equipped, were completed at the new Camp Alice on May 27, 1916. The dining room was pure tourism. Large enough to accommodate 250 guests at one time, it also had a lunch counter and a souvenir stand of rustic design.

The porch roof was supported by columns of logs which had been cut from wood on the mountain. Not designed for a hotel, this was a sightseer's house that could accommodate from 75 to 100 guests who might wish to spend the night on the mountain and view the striking scenery. Camp Alice was apparently named for the cook, Alice Padgett.

A special problem for accurately tracing the railroad's routing is that the former names and proper spelling of many of the feature mountains in the Blue Ridge and Black Mountain range have been changed, sometimes more than once. Bearwallow Knob was once called "Bearwallow Mountain;" Big Tom and Mount Craig were once "the Black Brothers." The present Clingmans Peak was once named "Mount Mitchell," and the present-day Mount Mitchell was once itself called "Clingmans Peak" or "Mount Clingman." Geographer Arnold Guyot referred to it as "Black Dome." Potato Knob was sometimes called "Potato Top," and Black Mountain Gap used to be called "Swannanoa Gap." In addition to spelling changes previously cited, Mount Hallback seems to have been spelled "Mount Haulback," and Mount Gibbes was spelled "Mount Gibbs." Puzzling but picturesque.

A change in spelling was often only the geographer's interpretation of the proper name. In many instances, the proper name may have been misspelled. Other times the Board of Geographic Names changed the spelling, such as dropping apostrophes, and so on. In general, the B.G.N. used local surveys to verify feature names. The reasons for changes are difficult to determine. This is only a sampling of the changes in the last 150 years, and others are too numerous to identify.

The logging railroad went deeper into the forests, but the scenic passenger railroad line claims our attention. On one of my trips to Camp Alice, I recorded an elevation there of 5,759 feet; however, the USGS and TVA figure is 5,789 feet above sea level. I missed their figure by only 30 feet, using both electronic altimeters, and a camper's altimeter.

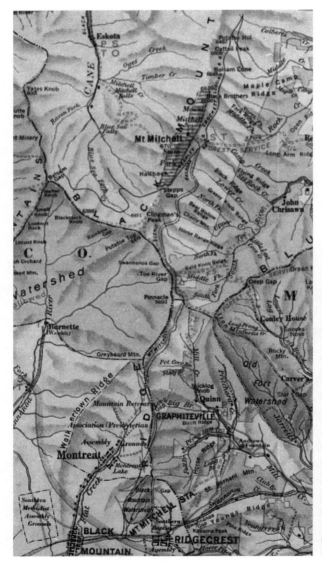

The Mount Mitchell Scenic Railroad ran in a northerly direction from the Mount Mitchell Station to Camp Alice, near the foot of Mount Mitchell. The Perley and Crockett Logging Railroad followed this same route, then extended past Camp Alice, where it ran westward to Balsam Gap and northeast along the eastern flank of the Black Mountains beyond Potato(e) Hill, and then back south near the foot of Balsam Cone. (Norfolk-Southern Archives)

The Logging Days

The first trees were felled on June 20, 1912, and the logging crews were busy preparing them to be hauled from the mountains as soon as the work was completed on the rail line.

In 1913 two hundred men of varied background performed the laborious task of cutting trees, loading logs, and transporting timber to the sawmill. Some of them were Austrian, but the majority were from Virginia, Tennessee, or the Carolinas.

Logging camps were in operation by 1915 at Commissary Ridge and just below Clingmans Peak. George Meyers and J.W. Sturgill were the supervisors. They were cutting all spruce and balsam trees from four to eight inches in diameter for pulpwood and shipping them to the Champion Fiber Company at Canton, N.C. All logs from eight inches up were cut into lumber at the sawmill.

The cut lumber was stacked about 12 feet high near the present Interstate 40 overpass at Black Mountain, drypacked in piles. At one time, there were hundreds of stacks behind the sawmill. The trestle that was located over present I-40 at Black Mountain, about 15 feet high, had upright timbers that were made of spruce, 12 × 12 inches wide, and 14 feet high. The railroad used oak and locust ties on the trestle, which was dual gauge. Most of the spikes on the main line were about four inches long, except near spurs or switches; the switch spikes were usually about six inches long.

The photographs of the trestle show its curved span from near the Southern Railway tracks to the junction of the present Old Toll Road.

The Mount Mitchell Railroad was filmed for millions of moving picture enthusiasts on August 20, 1914. Pictures were to be used in the Universal Weekly. It was repeated in the *Asheville Citizen* that Secretary N. Buckner of the local Board of Trade, together with F.L. Plaisance of the moving picture business, left on the morning of August 20 to head for the top of the mountain, where they would make the film.

Another event took place when more motion pictures of the logging operation on Mount Mitchell were shown, for the first time, at the Grove Park Inn on the night of June 12, 1916. The movies were made when the Applachian Logging Congress made a special visit to Mount Mitchell as the guests of the Clyde Iron Works and Perley and Crockett. Besides showing pictures of the logging operations in progress, there was a feature presentation about the operation of one of the giant skidders. These films attracted public attention. Finally, on October 4, 1916, a special trip was made to Mount Mitchell by Kenneth Spear, who made travelogue films for the Metro Corporation. The autumn leaves were a riot of colors, and several thousand feet of film recorded the scene along the road that zigzagged to the summit. Hundreds of sightseers were drawn to the top of the peak. Do the films still exist? Nobody knows. I did, however, attempt to locate them.

Tourism remained tempting, according to the *Asheville Citizen*, and by September 1915, plans were made to build a hotel on the slopes of Mount Mitchell. To be situated on Point Lookout, the structure would contain 50 rooms and be thoroughly modern, with hot and cold running water in every room, private baths, and electric lights.

Natural disaster intervened with the great flood of 1916. "The damage to the Mount Mitchell Railroad," Perley recalled afterward, "was slight. Of course it looked serious for a time while the waters were coming down the mountain and many logs were carried away and piles of timber overturned. The most serious damage we have sustained is the temporary interruption to our business and the filling up of our mill pond. We are busy today getting out an order for the Southern Railway, for timbers to be used in rebuilding trestles. We feel satisfied that our total loss will not exceed $2,000.... We are ready for tourist operations now."

The train crews and loggers were colorful personalities. One of the locomotive engineers was Little John Allison. Another notorious Mount Mitchell Railroad engineer was James Oliver Burgin, nicknamed "Big Jim." One of the foremen was Wallace Gragg; another was Will Padgett.

I interviewed the late James Willard Biddix, son of one of the overhead skidder operators, on August 3, 1990. Mr. Biddix's father operated a skidder on the railroad until he was no longer able to work. Mr. Biddix himself spent many a day on the railroad line. He told me that "the skidder was so loud, it could be heard for miles." Incidentally, his father took care of Mr. Perley's personal automobile, too. They were the best of friends and went on many hunting trips and walks together. Squirrels were usually their game on hunting trips.

Biddix told me that "people from all over brought in their cattle and turned them loose on the mountains." The cattle kept the undergrowth and weeds down to a minimum. Their owners brought them salt about once a week. A single herd would consist of over 500 head. The owners apparently had permits to do this. The cattle kept the land clean and kept the snakes away. Trains were sometimes detained while cattle were moved off the tracks. Usually, the locomotives left the mill, heading up the mountain before daybreak. Even when the engineers had no cause to blow their whistles, they did so anyway, frequently waking up the whole valley long before breakfast.

A number of black workers served as lumberjacks, cutting timber and working on the mountain. Several died from carelessness or from fighting between each other. They had been brought in on Southern Railway passenger trains.

Some of the loggers were of Italian descent, and it was reported that a handful of these men deceptively felled trees on each other. It was said that some were killed from arguing; however, I found nothing to substantiate this.

Train accidents occurred frequently, Biddix recalled, and there were fatalities. Perley kept a crew going all the time to put engines and cars back on the tracks. Biddix recalled that "if a brakeman hadn't lost a couple of fingers, he was considered inexperienced."

On June 9, 1914, Nat Grier, age 32, was caught between coupler blocks between two logging cars. Crushed on the left side of his body, he died from his injuries the next day. That was a disastrous month for safety; a few days later, Rufus Slemp, age 28, was standing by a loaded log car, when the log chains snapped and an enormous log crushed him against a bank. He was brought to the old Merriwether Hospital in Asheville in critical condition. It is doubtful that he survived either.

And then there was unexplained violence around the 1st of January 1915, when the white bronze monument dedicated to Prof. Elisha Mitchell, located at Mount Mitchell's summit, was destroyed. Sources of the *Asheville Citizen* reported it was dynamited. Motive and perpetrators were unknown. An employee of the Perley and Crockett Lumber Company, while cutting timber on Mount Mitchell, heard the explosion, but he attributed it to a prank by some of the workers. The next morning, however, coming in sight of the spot where the monument should have been, the workmen found it missing.

The original investigation showed that dynamite had been carefully placed at the base of the monument. It was thought by some that the blast, an act of revenge, was committed by foreigners who were in the employ of the lumber company and were dissatisfied with some act of the foreman. No other motive was ever found. For twenty-six years the statue had kept silent guard over the remains of the man who had made North Carolina aware that the state possessed the highest point of land east of the Mississippi.

But surprises were in store. The headline in the *Asheville Citizen* of Thursday, May 20, 1915, read, "MITCHELL MONUMENT WAS NOT DYNAMITED." The state investigating commission determined that the wind did the work. Anyone who is familiar with the effects of a dynamite explosion would have had to agree that there was no dynamite explosion. All evidence, indeed, pointed to that conclusion.

For over ten years, souvenir hunters broke away small pieces of the second section of the monument. People from almost every state had written and cut their names on the monument, each time removing a portion. These damages were heightened even more by someone who had placed a double-bladed ax into the center of the monument, leaving a great tear in its side. All this was captured in an old song familiar in that time:

It's a long hike to old Mount Mitchell, it's a long way to go.
It's a long hike to old Mount Mitchell, to the highest peak I know.
Good-bye old Mount Mitchell, farewell land so fair.
It's a long, long way to old Mount Mitchell, but my name's up there.

Governor Craig announced on July 17, 1915, that he was going to name a special commission to erect a monument to the memory of Professor Elisha Mitchell, to be located at the summit of the mountain after North Carolina had acquired a section of Mount Mitchell for a park. Governor Craig declared that "the monument should be as perpetual as the mountain itself and should be constructed in such form as to permit travelers to ascend to the top of it and, standing above the surrounding timber, command a view of the whole horizon of vast and lofty mountain ranges of impressive grandeur." Governor Craig spoke again about the scenic possibilities of Mount Mitchell in an interview on January 13, 1916. "In Mount Mitchell," he said, "Asheville and the state have an asset whose magnitude we have never yet realized.... The highest mountain east of the Mississippi, and with a railroad to the top of it, is something we should all be proud of and endeavor to exploit as much as possible." He also added that it was his hope "to see built on top of Mount Mitchell a really handsome and substantial monument to Dr. Elisha Mitchell."

Perley and Crockett announced on September 23, 1915, that they would construct an observation tower at the summit of the peak, capable of accommodating about fifty people at one time.

News happened fast concerning Mount Mitchell and its railroad in 1915. That was one of the most successful years for the tourist railroad line. The demand for tickets was phenomenal during the month of August in 1915. This forced Perley and Crockett to build several more passenger cars for the railroad line, and Passenger Agent Sandford H. Cohen announced that they would increase their excursions to four trips a week.

Ten new passenger cars were finished for the Mount Mitchell Railroad by the first week of April, 1916, representing the latest type of observation coaches of their time. Equipped with all the modern safety devices of those days, the cars, because of the peculiar construction of the Mount Mitchell Railroad, were rather short, and could carry 30 to 40 passengers. The unusually wide windows swung upward to the ceiling, giving ample observation space, yet the passengers were protected from rain.

Making the journey from Camp Alice was much easier in 1916 than it had been the previous year. Perley and Crockett had the trail rerouted to bypass the hard climb during the previous year. Also, the distance was shorter, about a quarter-mile long.

Mr. Perley wrote a letter to Albert Bauman, of the Mount Mitchell Forest Protective Association, on April 3, 1916, granting permission to use the railroad to get back and forth over the territory. He was told he would "ride at his own risk," and therefore, "assume all responsibility of an accident while using the railroad."

On top of the mountain, an observation tower was being constructed, according to the *Asheville Citizen,* which, "would reach high above the surrounding trees and afford an unobstructed view of the most beautiful mountain panorama in all this wide world. "Success and trouble, however, seem to go hand in hand. In 1917, when America was actively drawn into World War I, there were difficulties for the firm of Perley and Crockett. Judge Henry P. Lane issued an **instanter capias** order to force Perley and Crockett to comply with an earlier court judgment that they pay $600 and court costs for violating a statute

Early wooden observation tower built by Perley and Crockett at the summit of Mount Mitchell. (Biddix)

concerning the cutting of timber near the Asheville Watershed. They were supposed to let any and all timber lie within a 400-foot boundary of the watershed. The watershed was also badly impaired by the effects of fires that had been set out along the railroad. This was not the first offense for Perley and Crockett either. Their case was pending in Federal Court for being involved in damaging the watershed in 1916. That forest fire would cost the railroad firm $5,000 in a lawsuit. Dark days were in prospect.

The Destruction of the Forest

Much of the timber on Mount Mitchell and many acres beyond were in fact logged and destroyed by the hands of man for profit, a record which disheartened many people including Governor Locke Craig of North Carolina. Only a four-acre tract at the summit of the mountain had been spared of the axemen. Sam Foreman's report, "Lumbering in Montreat," noted that "mudslides prevailed; erosion and windfalls mar the summit of Mount Mitchell, all of which were serious alone, without being combined. But to make matters worse, the remaining surrounding trees were threatened even more so.... The forest decreased in size even more when fires started from the sparks given off by the engines. Never causing widespread fires, it did make scars that can still be seen along the unused part of the grade above Pot Cove Gap."

One fire on Mount Mitchell on July 8, 1914, destroyed $10,000 worth of timber near the summit. This particular fire was started by sparks from a locomotive igniting the dry leaves. Most of the engines were equipped with several different kinds of spark arrestors; however, they were either not maintained properly or they were not always in use.

Perley and Crockett's eastern section was already over halfway logged by 1915. Only a fraction of the virgin timber was saved from the axemen. A few of the areas did reforest themselves, but to a lesser degree. Camp Alice was one of those areas that, instead, turned into a grassy meadow. In places where the soil was not washed away, a small species of cherry, called fire cherry by the lumbermen, reproduced. However, this died down in a few years.

The *Asheville Citizen* reported that "Senator Weaver introduced on January 12, 1915, a bill for the creation of the "Mitchell Park Commission" for the special purpose of procuring through purchase, or condemnation proceedings, the summit of Mount Mitchell, to be used as a park for the people of the state. The park was to include the site of the Mitchell monument that was destroyed. An appropriation of

Picture of Governor Locke Craig taken in 1912.

$20,000 was made as the maximum amount to be expended in purchase of the lands and expenses of the commission.

Locke Craig, governor of North Carolina from 1913 to 1917 and a resident of Buncombe County since 1883, had spent much time in the North Fork Valley over the years and had regularly made trips to the Black Mountains and Mount Mitchell. Like others, Craig considered Mount Mitchell and the surrounding forest as a sacred place, not to be destroyed by the hand of man. In an address before the North Carolina Forestry Association in January 1915, he declared, "It was on a place like this [Mount Mitchell] that Moses communed with God, who revealed Himself to man. He has given this sacred place to us, and we should do our best to preserve it, and own it for herself and for her citizens forever."

Governor Craig understood that the lumber company, which had purchased practically all of the spruce timber on the Black Mountains including Mount Mitchell, had a legal right to both destroy the forest and burn over the land. Although a man in a city is prohibited, by law, from setting fire to his house, for the danger of destroying adjoining property, a man owning forest land is permitted to burn this land over, even though the burning might cause the destruction of the soil, flooding of farms below after heavy rains, and the destruction of other property. The law was not very protective against environmental damage.

In his speech to the American Forestry Association, Governor Craig said, "I tell you, the lumbermen—and I am not criticizing them, but us—the lumbermen are destroying North Carolina. We cannot expect them to sacrifice their business for the public good. They have bought that timber. They are entitled to every stick of it. If the people of North Carolina want to save it, they must do so. They cannot expect the lumbermen to save it; they must save it themselves. They must save it from the fires that follow the lumberman. If I can lend any mite of influence to this movement for the protection of our forests, I will do it; for in the protection of our forests, we are protecting the fields, we are protecting the place where crops must grow, and where men and women must grow in North Carolina; we are protecting the whole state."

The senate passed the Weaver bill to appropriate $20,000 for the purchase of the summit of Mount Mitchell on February 22, 1915. This was after a lengthy debate; attempts were made by Senator Muse to cut the appropriation to $12,500. Governor Craig reported the names of the members of the special commission on March 31, 1915, for purchasing the summit of Mount Mitchell and preserving its native forest for use as a state park. The names of the commission members appointed by the Governor were: G.T. Deyton, Green Mountain, Yancey County; W.F. Watson, Burnsville, Yancey County; M.C. Huneycutt, Burnsville; Wilson Hensley, Ball Creek, Yancey County; and T. Edgar Blackstock, Asheville.

Governor Craig visited Mount Mitchell on July 14, 1915. He and his party were delighted with the grandeur of scenes glimpsed from the train and from the summit of the peak. They declared upon their return that the day had been spent in a most enjoyable manner. While on the top of Mount Mitchell, Governor Craig visited portions of the tract which were to be purchased by the commonwealth as a state park.

In appreciation of Governor Locke Craig's efforts for the preservation of Mount Mitchell, the highest peak of the "Black Brothers," which is the second highest point in the eastern United States (elevation 6,647 feet), was named Mount Craig.

The announcement was made that the State of North Carolina had finalized the proposal to buy the Mount Mitchell area at a price of $5.00 an acre on November 13, 1915. In fact, all land desired for park pur-

View of Mount Mitchell from Mount Craig taken in 1916. (Norfolk-Southern Archives)

Same view from Mount Craig taken by the author on August 5, 1991. Clouds lingered for most of the day.

poses, 500 acres, with the exception of the five-acre Connaly tract at the summit, was offered at a nominal cost to the state. Perley and Crockett helped to reforest the area in the late 1920s by contributing more than 100,000 seedlings of fraser fir, red spruce, and an introduced species, Norway spruce.

Timbering Near its End—
The Railroad Opens to Passengers

Long before the state park existed, Fred Perley and William Crockett carried special groups of passengers on their logging railroad. They had no desire to end their logging business, but they realized that operating a scenic passenger railroad would serve a dual purpose by profiting tourism and Perley and Crockett. Passengers were transported from just east of the town of Black Mountain to the terminus of the scenic railroad at Camp Alice, right below the summit of Mount Mitchell.

By 1914 Perley and Crockett had built three crude passenger coaches, which were operated on a limited basis. The trial excursions convinced Perley and Crockett that continuing passenger service would be successful and not interfere with the logging operations.

According to *The Historical Foundation News*, Perley and Crockett's somewhat primitive homemade passenger cars were boarded at a platform by the Southern Railway's lines close to the mill where the logs were sawed into lumber. Arrangements were also made to receive and discharge passengers to and from Mount Mitchell at or above Montreat, as some of the old-timers who used it can testify.

A 1917 advertising pamphlet glowingly described the trip: "Switchbacks cunningly constructed by an unexcelled feat of engineering make the ascent gentle and pleasant.... Mount Mitchell Railroad zigzags up the mountainside, spans mountain gorges and ravines, and climbs almost to the tip of the majestic monarch of them all...."

One passenger was ecstatic: "Going through the heart of the mountains over steep grades and around winding curves, the railroad carries travelers to a point where the panorama is most inspiring and the scenic beauties are unsurpassed."

Another proclaimed it as "the grandest mountain scenic country in America. Thousands have taken the trip, and hundreds who have visited

Switzerland and the Rockies declare with enthusiasm that there is no mountain scenic trip in the world that surpasses the trip to Mount Mitchell.''

Another witness swore: "Hikers forget their weariness and declare they would abandon the comforts of civilization and walk miles to see again the panorama of clouds and lights that make up the vista from the tower of Mount Mitchell. Shading from a dusky blue to a dark green, the unending hills form an awe inspiring view, while clouds below and above add an element of variability to the scene. And then at sunrise or sunset, the sky is sprayed with brilliant hues that for a moment gilds the surrounding peaks with a Midas-like touch, and the beauty from Mount Mitchell lingers on in the minds of all who have once viewed this awe inspiring scene." Who could ask for anything more?

Still another passenger said: "The railway that threads its way for a distance of twenty-one miles, almost to the summit, unrolls the eye to a scenic vista of surpassing beauty, a panorama to which few tongues or pens can do full justice.''

A man on the train wryly summed up such encomiums: "It would bankrupt the English language to try and describe the trip to Mount Mitchell.''

Col. Sandford H. Cohen was hired as General Passenger Agent and for railroad promotions, an excellent choice for the job. He had past experience promoting tourism by serving as manager of the Greater Western North Carolina Association, an agency promoting tourism in western North Carolina. He had also developed the Isle of Palms in South Carolina. More than anybody else, Cohen was responsible for launching the new era of tourism beginning then in the Black Mountains.

Colonel Cohen's promotions paid off by luring tourists to the Mount Mitchell Scenic Railroad from the entire eastern United States. He printed pamphlets, sold souvenir booklets, and ran full-page advertisements in the *Asheville Citizen*.

Even though the Mount Mitchell passenger railroad line operated on a limited basis for almost two years, the dedication and formal opening were not scheduled until July 16, 1915. Newspaper reporters, officials, and many other persons were on hand for the official inauguration and excursion ride to near the summit of Mount Mitchell.

President Fairfax Harrison of the Southern Railway made the trip to Mount Mitchell in late July of 1915, declaring that "the construction of the mountain road was a marvelous feat of engineering.''

The Mount Mitchell Railroad prompted Harrison to construct the Mount Mitchell Station at the interchange of the two railroads just east of the town of Black Mountain. A convenient connection schedule was established with the Southern Railway to Asheville, enabling visitors to Mount Mitchell to stay overnight at a wide variety of accommodations in rapidly growing Black Mountain. Harrison predicted that the "Mount Mitchell Station will add to the attractions of mountain travel and will draw hundreds of people who have for many years cherished the hope of reaching the top of Mount Mitchell."

The first all-rail trip from Asheville to the Mount Mitchell Station via Southern Railway, and from the station to Camp Alice, near the summit of Mount Mitchell, was run by the Mount Mitchell Scenic railroad on August 3, 1915. This was chosen as "Asheville Day," to celebrate the acquisition of the summit for the new state park and to commemorate the official opening of the passenger train service. All participants were invited to the complimentary dinner on Mount Mitchell, served by the Asheville Board of Trade. Seating was limited to 200 so it was necessary, for those who wished to go, to get tickets early.

Depending on the weather, the Mount Mitchell Railroad used as many as seven passenger cars to carry a maximum of 250 people to Camp Alice on each run. On each trip, the train carried a conductor, an engineer, a fireman, and two or three brakemen. The train departed from Mount Mitchell Station at 9:40 a.m. and took three hours to travel the 21 miles to Camp Alice. For reasons of safety, the return trip took three and one-half hours, with the train arriving at Mount Mitchell Station at 6:47 p.m. The cost of the round trip from Mount Mitchell Station to Camp Alice was $2.50, only half of what it had been during the railroad's experimental operations the previous year. To provide for interest and orientation along the route, identifying signs were placed at more than 20 locations. Passengers were refreshed and entertained with drinks, candy, souvenirs, booklets, and personal photographs.

Camp Alice, the end of the tourist railroad line, was completed by Perley and Crockett on May 27, 1916. Today, Camp Alice is in a state of disrepair. Only an occasional hiker or hunter uses the rocky trail.

At least 15,000 people visited Mount Mitchell in 1915 and 1916, by way of the Mount Mitchell Railroad. Over 1,000 people made the trip in one week alone during 1916. Not since the 1850s when William Patton's mountain house attracted visitors to the Black Mountains had a tourist enterprise in the range been so successful. Cohen rejoiced at the response the railroad line had generated from his intensive advertising campaign: "I have been connected with many enterprises, but none that was as easy to attract attention to as the Mount Mitchell road. Everyone who takes the trip becomes an advertiser, thus making the promotion of it an easy task."

There was little exchange between the tourists and the loggers, whose headquarters at that time was at Commissary Ridge. The operation of Camp Alice was leased to H. Russell Cohen, who is thought to have been a nephew of Sandford Cohen.

When the passengers finished their lunch at Camp Alice, most of them took advantage of the improved trail leading up to the summit of the mountain. Since the trail had been shortened to less than a quarter-mile, the walk was quite easy.

A controversy arose in 1917 when the North Carolina State Corporation Commission charged that Perley and Crockett's Mount Mitchell Railroad was charging more than the state rate of two and one-half cents a mile for passengers riding their excursion trains. Lawyers for Perley & Crockett denied by countering that "the state commission had no jurisdiction over the railroad, and that the commission so stated it before the road undertook to carry passengers." Mr. Martin (one of the attorneys for Perley & Crockett) pointed out that the Mount Mitchell Railroad operated on private property, every foot of the road being on ground leased or owned by Perley & Crockett, owners of the road, and that it was a scenic railroad, operated to carry persons from one point on privately owned property to another point on property owned by the same parties. He contended that the road was not a common carrier and did not come under the rules governing common carriers. He also deplored "such an attack on one of the most attractive, valuable, and widely known points of interest in Western North Carolina."

An interesting event took place on August 3, 1918, when passengers hoping to ride to Mount Mitchell were blocked by a train wreck on the Southern Railway, just beyond Swannanoa. The tourists did not let that stop them. Learning that automobiles could be used to get to Mount Mitchell Station and still not miss the train, they hired several automobile companies, and 80 people rode cross-country to catch the excursion train to Mount Mitchell.

By 1918, the Mount Mitchell Railroad had become one of the most famous tourist stops in the eastern United States. Passengers could enjoy the ride to Camp Alice, continue on the smooth trail to the summit of

Mount Mitchell, and finally view the spectacular scenes from the new observation tower built by Perley and Crockett and completed in April of 1916.

But far away in Europe, World War I was swelling to its bloody climax, toppling empires and sending deaths and casualties into the millions as American doughboys fell by the thousands. Every aspect of American life was affected by the war effort. The United States Railroad Administration coordinated the nation's railway network, even producing excellent locomotive designs which remained classic into the 1950s.

The War Department urged the owners of the Mount Mitchell Railroad to suspend passenger operations on August 24, 1918. The government wanted to step up logging production so that the lumber could be used in making planes and ships for the war. Using the locomotives for carrying passengers put a drain on the already low fuel supplies, and it interfered with engines that were needed in the logging camps to haul logs. Perley and Crockett agreed to shut down the excursions temporarily, feeling a sense of duty to do so. The public was very disappointed with the closing of the passenger operation on the Mount Mitchell Railroad. It was the beginning of what would be a permanent abandonment.

A new record was made in July 1918 for the amount of passengers visiting the peak by way of the Mount Mitchell Railroad. Twenty-five percent more people traveled in July of 1918 than in the same month in 1917.

The Mount Mitchell Railroad had its best and its worst year in 1918. A woman named Lula J. Howie sued Perley and Crockett for an injury sustained while she was trying to get off the train. The train was apparently derailed in early July, and when the lady attempted to get down from the train, she fell, while the official was busy doing something else besides helping her off the car. It was said that she sustained severe and permanent injuries. She sued the railway company for $25,000.

The next death bell rang for the Mount Mitchell Railroad on June 24, 1919. Perley and Crockett revealed the news that the passenger service would be discontinued. The owners of the road wanted to use their railroad for hauling timber only. Calls from tourists around the country came flooding in. They all wondered when the trips would restart so that they could plan their vacations. There was apparently a deluge of letters to Sandford Cohen and Fred Perley, who must have had many regrets about the closing.

Since the railroad planned to discontinue the passenger service, there was no need for Camp Alice to remain open, so it ceased operations. With the closing of the Mount Mitchell passenger railroad, there came a strong demand for an easy means of access to the high peak. Many pressed for the reopening of the railroad, but this was not to be.

Logging operations were completed by August 15, 1921. After the logging was finished, there were measures under consideration to operate the railroad for passenger use for the balance of the season. A large amount of pulpwood was to be hauled during September and October, and the Champion Fiber Company was still cutting pulpwood on the boundary, which would not interfere with passenger operation of the line. This was to be the last week that the firm of Perley and Crockett would cut any more timber.

On Friday, August 26, 1921, a party including Lieutenants Runser and Turner, of the U.S. Air Service, and Major J. Hampton Rich left Asheville for the summit of Mount Mitchell to investigate whether there was a possibility of a landing field on the highest mountain east of the Mississippi. A place 600 feet long and 150 feet wide adaptable for a landing field and with a slant suitable for a runway was found due west from the flagstaff, a short distance below the summit. But the possibility apparently was not carried through. After the timber had been cut in the vicinity of Mount Mitchell and the railway ceased to be operated for logging purposes, the lumber company promised to make a turnpike along the track of the railway.

Development of the Shay and Climax Engines

What kinds of motive power did the Mount Mitchell logging railroad use? Chiefly Shay and Climax locomotives. Employed on many logging railroads in difficult terrain, these geared locomotives differed sharply from other steam engines. They had a picturesque and distinctive appearance and, in spite of their wide use, are not too well known to the general public, though they are fairly familiar to railroad enthusiasts.

The Mount Mitchell railroad was a picturesque sight in very scenic country, and its locomotives were just as picturesque, as we enable this notable railroad to live again. The panting chug and whistling of the log/passenger trains can still be heard, if we only use the ears of our imagination.

Ephraim Shay of Haring, Michigan, conformed the existing gear precept to operate a swiveled truck on a steam locomotive and to convey that energy to other trucks by using pliant drive shafts and gears. Though the characteristics of Shay's locomotive were already known then, he still acquired a patent for his invention by forming a new combination of already existing components.

Since he would not apply for a patent right away, about 10 Shay-type locomotives were constructed by other manufacturers. Four of them were built by the Lima Machine Works of Lima, Ohio (which was later known as the Lima Locomotive and Machine Works).

In 1881, Shay and James Henderson of Michigan Iron Works combined their knowledge to create geared locomotives that towered above anything Lima would construct until years later. However, in 1883, the Michigan Iron Works went bankrupt, and only six of these unique locomotives were constructed. In the early 1880s geared-locomotive excitement was uncontrollable in Michigan. Ephraim Shay's first crude locomotive was built in 1877 at William Crippen's Cadillac City Iron Works in Michigan. Little else is known about Crippen's vague role in the history of the Shay Locomotive.

Early Shay locomotives may have been crude and ungainly, to say the least, but they got the job done. Their chief feature—it was unmistakable—was that their gear mechanism and cylinders were on one side only, giving them a lopsided appearance.

Lima used a four-letter classification system to designate Shays, as shown by the following table:

CLASS	CYLINDERS	TRUCKS
A	2	2
B	3	2
C	3	3
D	3	4

The range of sizes of Shays was wide, from 10 to 150 tons, but only a few 150-ton monsters were produced. The last Shay was built by Lima in 1945, and the total of all Shays constructed was 2770.

The Shay locomotive is able to pull a passenger coach to a maximum speed of about eight miles per hour, but compensating for grades, curvatures, size of cars or engines, and other factors could change this rule.

At first, the Shay locomotive was little more than a vertical boiler and a two-cylinder engine mounted at one side of a flat bed on two four-wheel trucks. A water tank, wood bin, and canopy completed the super-structure. Flexible couplings in the drive shaft of the running gear allowed the trucks to swivel and to accommodate themselves to uneven tracks. Another way of describing the running gear would be to say that the driving rods turned the line of shafts and universal joints, including beveled gears that sent the power to the wheels of at least two or more swiveling trucks.

When the Lima Machine Works took over construction of Shay's locomotive, it quickly improved; a horizontal boiler was added (off-center, which only added to the lopsided appearance). The Shay grew to three cylinders and three trucks and eventually even to four-truck models.

The distinction of making plans for another geared locomotive, the Climax, went to Charles D. Scott. He had observed the superiority of steam power on a tram road he had built in Spartansburg, Pennsylvania, around 1875. Because Scott's geared locomotive was made by the Climax Manufacturing Company of Corry, Penna., it came to be known by the Climax name. The locomotive used gears to power the axles of its trucks, but these gears were placed at the center of each axle. Originally, a differential not unlike those on modern automobiles and so-called "loose wheels" facilitated passage around curves. These devices caused a loss of power when negotiating curves on steep grades and were abandoned.

Although Scott was undoubtedly the inventor, a patent was applied for on February 10, 1888, and granted on December 4, 1888, to George D. Gilbert, who had worked on its design and had drawn up the patent application. In 1889, the president of the Climax Manufacturing Company, Rush S. Battles, a lawyer, applied for additional patents, thus deepening the mystery surrounding the locomotive's invention. It was not until 1892 that Charles D. Scott was acknowledged as the true inventor, and then only after he had sued both Gilbert and Battles.

Like the first Shays, the early Climax locomotives had a vertical boiler and a two-cylinder marine engine. They were on a flat bed supported by a pair of four-wheel trucks. Over the years, the Climax passed through many changes in appearance. The vertical boiler was replaced by a round firebox tee-boiler. This gave way to a square firebox tee-boiler and, subsequently, to the choice of either a taper shell boiler or a straight shell boiler. Because it had a squarish wood frame, the Climax came to be known as the "Box Car Engine." Logging-train crews liked it because of the shelter afforded by its large cab. Engineers preferred it because it was equipped with a two-speed gear selector giving a choice of high and low speeds, plus a free-wheeling neutral position. Its comparatively low price and the simplicity of its design, together with the ease with which repairs could be made, ensured that it would be a favorite with logging railroads.

Climax locomotives were offered in three models, referred to in the catalog as Class A, Class B, and Class C. Class A locomotives ranged from 12- to 22-ton sizes. Class B locomotives lacked the gear-shift feature and ranged in size from 17 to 62 tons. On these the position of the cylinders was changed to an angle of about 25 degrees. This tilt of the cylinder was a feature of Class B Climaxes, making them instantly recognizable. Class C locomotives could be had in weights from 70 to 100 tons. The first Class C Climax was a 50-ton model built in 1897 for the Colorado & Northwestern Railway. It was later used in the construction of the White Pass & Yukon Route. Evidently it was not too successful, because no other three-truck Climax locomotive was built until 1903.

The second three-truck locomotive was built for the Casper, South

Fork & Eastern Railroad in California. It was a 65-ton model, and shortly thereafter 75- and 85-ton locomotives were built by Climax. The weights were later standardized at 70-, 80-, and 90-tons. The first 100-ton Class C Climax was completed for display at the Pacific Logging Conference. It was sold to the Buckley Logging Company of Eagle Gorge, Washington. Eventually, 17 sizes of Climax locomotives were available. After 1911, the main frames were offered in steel as an option, and eventually wood frames were dropped. In all, about 1,100 Climax locomotives were constructed before the last one was finished in 1928 (for the Forest Commission of Melbourne, Australia).

Of the approximately 1,200 Climax locomotives built, only 19 are known to still exist. Many were scrapped in the 1930s, as most North Carolina logging companies worked out their forests at that time or went bankrupt due to the Depression. The few that remained were cut up for World War II scrap drives or disposed of shortly thereafter.

Many years of research by several noted historians show that only four narrow gauge logging locomotives escaped the scrapper's torch in North Carolina. We all keep hoping someone, someday, will discover another one in some long forgotten place. It's like a search for buried treasure or a lost gold mine. With persistence, and faith, one day perhaps....

Perley and Crockett's Locomotives

Walter Casler worked for Climax Locomotive Company for nearly nine years. The last four years he was a traveling engineer delivering new engines. He grew up with Climax from the time he was a small boy. His father worked for Climax for many years. And when he was old enough, he too went to work for Climax. He later worked awhile for the Heisler Locomotive Works in Erie, Pennsylvania, and he was well versed on the Shays and other locomotives. The steam locomotive was his love and hobby ever since he was a boy. He was an expert especially on logging railroads. Perley and Crockett did have two Shays, but by the end of their operations, one was gone, either sold or moved to some other place.

The term, "construction number" (C.N.), widely used by railfans, means the same as shop number. However, shop number is the correct term to use, and the records of Lima on Shay, Heisler, Climax, and other builders always refer to the shop numbers. The term, "C.N.," an invention of the railfans in past years, has caught on. Mr. Casler worked for both Climax and Heisler, who always used an order number to charge all time and materials to for costing purposes, and Casler never heard of their using a "construction number." The shop number, which is actually the serial number, is used by the builder to record all that pertains to each locomotive or machine. The number becomes very important in later years, when it is necessary to order repair parts. The original specification sheets used in building the locomotive are filed in the office under the shop number for future reference.

Near the end of World War I, Lima set up a policy of having a number of agents, servicemen, etc., make periodic calls on all of the lumber companies as well as all other places using locomotives—possible sources of sale. Mr. Casler remembered that Climax Manufacturing Company had roadmen make visits to lumber companies and that they used to run into the Shay agents. Roaming around in every place, the Climax men not only reported data on the Shays, but they also often listed all the other makes of locomotives on the job.

These file cards today are a valuable source of data, but one does have to be careful in interpreting the data and not accept it as flawless. Mr. Casler found that the agents made many mistakes, not only on their competitors' engines, but also on their own Shays. Following is the data on the Mount Mitchell railroad motive power:

Dickey, Campbell and Company Shay Engine Number 1, Shop Number 2512, 36-inch gauge, 10 by 10 cylinders, 36-ton, 29 inch drivers was shipped March 13, 1912.

Dickey, Campbell and Company Shay Engine Number 2, Shop Number 2568, 36-inch gauge, 10 by 10 cylinders, 36-ton, 29 inch drivers shipped from Lima July 27, 1912.

Engine Number 3. This engine appears to have been a Climax, but there is no confirming data.

Engine Number 4. Climax. Seems to have been owned by Dickey and Campbell. Shop number is unknown. 36-inch gauge, 42-ton, date shipped not known.

Engine Number 5. Climax. Also seems to have been owned by Dickey and Campbell. Shop number 1235. 36-inch gauge, 42-ton, Class B. Record also states that this Climax locomotive was a duplicate of the Number 4 previously furnished by Climax. Contract dated August 1, 1913, and signed by C.A. Dickey, president.

Engine Number 6 appears to have been a Cooke 0-4-0 rod engine.

Engine Number 7 Climax Perley and Crockett. Shop number 1319, 36-inch gauge, 45-ton, Class B Climax locomotive. Contract dated August 14, 1914, signed by Fred A. Perley.

Engine Number 8 Climax Perley and Crockett. Shop number 1321, 36-inch gauge, 45-ton, Class B Climax locomotive. Contract dated September 1, 1914, signed by Fred A. Perley.

According to Lima's appraisal of the mechanical condition, they never said it was good on any of their competitors' engines. For instance, they say Numbers 4 and 5 are in bad condition. But this was not true. Mr. Casler knew these two Climax engines, and they went to other owners and saw hard service for many years after they left Black Mountain. Mr. Casler believed there were never three Shays there. He has Shay's original shipping records and the Shay book, which show no other Shays for Dickey and Campbell or Perley and Crockett.

Now to the Number 6; it shows on the Lima Service Card as Number

6 builder Cooke and a 2-6-0. However, it probably was not a 2-6-0. According to the Southern Iron & Equipment Company (SI&E Company), they sold it secondhand to Dickey and Campbell as Number 6 on February 12, 1913, and stated it was an 0-4-0. There is a picture of it in Michael Koch's book, **Steam and Thunder in the Timber,** which shows it as an 0-4-0. But the number, while identified as Number 6, does not look exactly like 6 but does resemble either 2, 3, or 8. So Mr. Casler could not corroborate it as Number 6, but perhaps it was.

Engine Number 5 left Perley and Crockett and went to Suncrest Lumber as Number 4 in Sunburst, N.C., and then to Blackwood Lumber as Number 5 in LaPort, N.C., and was supposedly converted to standard gauge.

Engines Number 2 Shay and Number 7 Climax after leaving Perley and Crockett appear to have gone to J. Natwick and Nixon Lumber Co. in Henckel, Virginia. According to SI&E Company sales, it shows the listing to sell to Dickey and Campbell Number 6/0-4-0 Cooke locomotive on February 12, 1913.

But a word of caution: Mr. Casler found that SI&E Company records were not always accurate in numerous cases. One thing that SI&E Company was notoriously sloppy in was their bookkeeping. Then a noxious railfan got into them, and he altered them to suit his own ideas. So the accuracy of these records cannot be guaranteed.

Casler was very doubtful that Number 6 was a Cooke-built locomotive. He also raises a question about its being Number 6. The record for the Climax Number 5 was not dated until August 1, 1913. And the Number 4 had to come before that date. The first two locomotives purchased and numbered were Shays Number 1 and Number 2, both dated as shipped from Lima Locomotive works in 1912. One was in July. So the problem is: why would the rod engine Number 6 be assigned Number 6 before they got the Climax Numbers 4 and 5? Now this so-called Number 6 was what is called a rod engine because it used side rods connected to the cross head, piston stem, and the driving wheels. They are also called "direct connected engines."

There could be a possibility that when Dickey and Campbell got this engine, the SI&E Company did not ship it to them from their Atlanta, Georgia, shop but shipped it from some other location and that they never repainted or lettered it. So the Number 6 could have been on it from its former owner. These secondhand dealers of locomotives in many cases were only agents selling used engines on commission for owners who had them to dispose of, and not all of them were first taken to Atlanta and overhauled before selling them.

Allen Paul researched much of the narrow gauge railroad topic between 1981 and 1983 for the U.S. Forest Service. During that period, he also supervised the restoration of the only narrow gauge Climax locomotive in existence in North America, excepting one very incomplete 36-inch gauge Class A Climax in Alaska. The locomotive his team restored is now on display at the Cradle of Forestry in America Museum in the Pisgah National Forest near Brevard, N.C. This locomotive is a Class B Climax shop number 1323, built in 1915 for Champion Fiber Company and operated as its Number 3 at Robbinsville, N.C., and Fires Creek, N.C. Shop number 1323 was sold in 1948 to the E.L.Y.-Thomas Lumber Company of Jettsville, West Virginia. It was retired in 1953 and sold to two private individuals in Ann Arbor, Michigan, in 1955, from whom the Forest Service purchased the locomotive in 1973. There are only three other known North Carolina narrow gauge logging steam locomotives still in existence.

Shop number 3314 operates on special occasions today at the Allaire, New Jersey, State Park near Farmington, N.J. The other two locomotives were side-rod steam locomotives. Shop number 4274 is now on display at the Edaville Tourist Railroad in South Carver, Massachusetts. Shop number 4776 is now on display on Main Street in Hardeeville, South Carolina.

The History of the Perley and Crockett Families

Allen Putnam Perley came to Williamsport, Penna., shortly after the Civil War from his home in Oldtown, Maine. At this time, Williamsport was known as the "Lumber City of the World." Mr. Perley prospered, became well known, and was able to obtain strong financial backing. He took a partner named William Howard, an Englishman, and formed the Howard & Perley Lumber Co.

But in June of 1889, a disaster struck. The lumber industry in the West Branch Valley was wiped out by a great flood from which it never fully recovered. When the mess was sorted out, Howard & Perley had no lumber, no sawmill, and worse yet, no logs. The boom had been full from the spring drives. The higher water broke the boom, and millions of board feet of timber floated toward Chesapeake Bay. However, the company had money and good credit and also owned the timber rights on Young Woman's Creed. Within the next couple of years they built a new sawmill at North Bend and a logging railroad into the timber and hired a jobber to stock the miller. They were back in the lumber business. Before the North Bend site was cut out, Howard made it known that when they were through there, he also was through as a lumberman.

A year or so after Allen Perley came to Williamsport, he returned to Maine and was married. He brought his wife back to Williamsport. Early in 1896, his second daughter married William H. (Bert) Crockett. About this time also, Mr. Perley was elected President of the West Branch Bank of Williamsport. He had also become active (behind the scenes) in Republican politics. Some years later he would become a Director of the Bell Telephone Company of Pennsylvania. He had no intention of leaving the lumber business, but, with Mr. Howard quitting the firm after North Bend was cut out, Perley needed a man who knew the lumber business and on whom he could rely. A clear cut choice was his son-in-law, Bert Crockett.

Photo of Fred A.
Perley, made at
Brock Studios
in   Asheville,
North Carolina.

William   H.
Crockett, Mr.
Perley's part-
ner. (Crockett)

Allen Perley's first son, Fred A. Perley, was then attending Lehigh University and later was graduated with a degree in Civil Engineering. At this time he had no interest in the lumber business. Upon graduation from Lehigh, he took a job in Washington, D.C., building bridges for the Federal Government.

Perley's second son, Allen P. Perley, Jr. entered Princeton University about 1901. "Budd" Perley was at Princeton several years when he, and the then-President of the University, Woodrow Wilson, had a disagreement. Budd's college career ended abruptly; he was sent home.

William H. (Bert) Crockett was born in Jersey Shore, Penna., in 1865. His father had moved from Calais, Maine, to this area before the Civil War. When Bert Crockett was about two years old, his father moved the family to Williamsport. Bert Crockett attended the local schools. While growing up, he became familiar with the Susquehanna River and the many sawmills along its banks. He also learned shorthand and typing. For some time he worked in the office of a miller there.

Then he decided to try his hand at selling. This went so well that he set up a partnership. Bert bought and sold the lumber while his partner ran the office. Things progressed well; the firm made money. However, about 1894, the partnership broke up from unknown causes. Bert Crockett went back to selling lumber for his own account, and in 1896 he married one of the daughters of Allen P. Perley.

When Budd Perley's Princeton days ended so abruptly, his father sent him to Allendale, Penna., to work under Bert Crockett and to learn the lumber business. This was naturally easy for him; he had been raised around sawmills and had worked during several summer vacations at Allendale. He knew what went in the front end of a mill and what came out the back.

In 1904 these men were in various places. Allen P. Perley was in Williamsport and occupied with the affairs of the West Branch Bank and his lumber interests. Bert Crockett and Budd Perley were busy in Allendale operating the A.P. Perley Lumber Company. Fred A. Perley was in Washington, D.C., busy as one of the engineers building the Connecticut Avenue Bridge. About this time, Fred married one of the daughters of Henry S. Mosser of Williamsport. Mr. Mosser owned a large tannery there and also one in Parsons, West Virginia.

Bert Crockett was sent from Allendale into West Virginia. There, probably with the help of Sam Slaymaker, he turned up with the Jenningston lumber project. After the timber had been cruised, arrangements were made to buy the property.

When his daughter married, Mr. Mosser had promised her that he would build her a house as part of her wedding gift. When he heard that they were moving to Jenningston, he instructed Fred to build the house at his expense. This was done. Early in 1907, Bert Crockett learned that there was a large amount of timber in Buchanan County, Virginia. He went into this area and decided on Honaker, Va., as his base of operations. After a good many months, the timber was bought. Bert could see by now that other timber, still unbought, would eventually come to this mill.

After the Honaker Lumber Company was formed, officials decided to build the mill several miles outside of Honaker. Budd Perley was sent to Honaker from Allendale, where the A.P. Perley Lumber Company was closed. The newly established mill town was named Putnam. Houses were built for the men and their families, a post office was added, followed by a company store, an ice plant, and a sawmill. Then a double band mill and a large pond were set up.

Budd Perley was made General Superintendent of this operation, and a house was built for him and his family. While the mill was being constructed, a logging railroad was extended into the timber. Sometime in 1908 the mill was in operation. For the next five years, Bert spent most of his time traveling between Williamsport, Penna.; Jenningston, W.Va.; and Putnam, Va.

The Honaker Lumber Company was an all-hardwood operation. A great deal of white and red oak and yellow poplar came to this mill. It was about 1917 before these woods were sawed out. Late in 1912 when the end of the Jenningston operation was in sight, Perley and Crockett began looking for new prospects, which led them to Black Mountain, N.C.

Bert Crockett had heard that a mill and timber rights were for sale at Black Mountain. The timber was all virgin spruce and stood on the slopes of Mount Mitchell. Since this is the highest mountain east of the Mississippi River, logging it would not be easy. The owners of the mill (Dickey and Campbell) had operated for a few years, cutting the hardwood off the lower slopes of the mountain. When they had attempted to extend their narrow-gauge logging railroad up the mountain into the spruce timber, they ran out of money and decided to sell out.

Perley and Crockett bought this operation, with all of its available equipment. They moved the Perley & Crockett Lumber Co. from

Jenningston, W.Va., to Black Mountain, N.C. Thus a partnership was set up between Fred Perley and Bert Crockett.

Frank Lundy was brought in from Jenningston to help with the extension of the rail line. Once the timber was reached, it became Lundy's job to run the grade lines for the spur tracks that were necessary to reach the rest of the timber with the equipment that was then in use.

By 1915 Perley and Crockett had added to their equipment in order to stock the mill. They now had about 20 miles of narrow gauge track. and an inventory of engines. Perley and Crockett continued this business until 1921, when the timber was cut out and the firm was disbanded.

William H. (Bert) Crockett was born in 1864 and died in 1952, at the age of 88. He is buried in the Wildwood Cemetery in Williamsport, Penna. Frederick A. Perley was born in 1876 and died in 1955, at the age of 79. He is buried in the Mountain View Memorial Park in Black Mountain, N.C.

The Takeover of the Railroad by Perley and Crockett

On September 27, 1913, Dickey, Campbell and Company, Inc. sold to Frederick A. Perley and William H. Crockett all of their milled lumber—about three million board feet stacked in its lumberyard located near the town of Black Mountain. They also sold all of the spruce and balsam left standing or on the ground. This tract was located at the head-waters of the Cane River.

Perley and Crockett continued their buying spree by purchasing several more tracts of land from Black Mountain to Yancey County, acquiring the buildings, sawmill, tools, right-of-ways, branches, switches, cars, engines, tools, machinery, and appliances used in construction. They apparently leased all of the 18 miles of track from Southern Railway. They purchased nearly all of the rolling stock, to boot. It was one of the biggest lumber "deals" in the history of North Carolina.

Dickey and Campbell must have been disheartened about the loss of their narrow gauge railroad to a point near Mount Mitchell, that they had worked so hard for, for two long years.

Perley & Crockett would continue operating the lumber camps, sawmill, and the railroad that Dickey and Campbell had enjoyed. Perley & Crockett ended up with six locomotives, 70 logging flats, two loaders, two steam skidders, 30 teams of horses, and 200 men who were working in the camps. This buyout probably cost Perley and Crockett more than a half-million dollars.

The Sawmill

The sawmill was located close to the Southern Railway tracks near Black Mountain. Just east of town, the interchange of the Mount Mitchell Railroad met with the Southern Railway main line coming out of Black Mountain. This interchange consisted of a short grade running down from the Southern Railway line. Since the interchange was dual gauge, it would accommodate both narrow and standard gauge rolling stock. A double band sawmill was constructed near this interchange, and 110,000 board feet of lumber could be sawed daily.

The mill and the plant were almost finished by June 21, 1912. The machinery was being hauled in and put in place, and the mill was scheduled for operation by July 1, 1912. However, it was delayed until August 1, 1912, because the track gang was still busy laying rails. The sawmill, the biggest one in this part of the country at that time, was constructed for about $50,000. Dickey and Campbell also desired to build a stave mill later on, so that by-products of the mill could be used.

After the logs were dumped into the mill pond, they were drawn up into the mill by a track that was built on piers almost throughout the length of the pond. A sheltered siding could easily accommodate four or five boxcars beside the mill. Twin smokestacks were positioned on the north side of the mill. The finished lumber was transported out of the mill on the interchange that connected with Southern Railway (formerly the Western North Carolina Railroad).

The mill was made by Clark Brothers of Rochester. One of the residents of Black Mountain recalled that the ''carriage on the saw moved so fast, that the men had to be belted to it.'' He further said that ''this could have been observed when the men set the dogs to grab the logs.''

Most of the trees were straight as an arrow, it was remarked, and from 100 to 125 feet in height with only a few limbs on the lower part.

The Beginning of a New Road—
The Mount Mitchell Toll Road

Certificates of incorporation for the Mount Mitchell Development Company, issued by the North Carolina secretary of state in Raleigh, were filed with John H. Cathey, clerk of the Superior court, on Wednesday, August 31, 1921. The company headquarters would be in Black Mountain, and the total amount of capital stock was set at $100,000, divided into 1,000 shares at the par value of $100 each. Following is the list of incorporators and the shares they held: C.A. Dickey, 490 shares; Fred A. Perley, 490 shares; R.E. Currier, 10 shares; and R.R. Dickey, 10 shares.

On September 15, 1921, condemnation proceedings were filed in the Superior court by the Development Company against the Mountain Retreat Association and W.H. Belk of Mecklenburg County. The court was requested to estimate the value of a right-of-way located on the lands of the Mountain Retreat Association, which followed the old Mount Mitchell Railroad. The Development Company wanted to build a turnpike to the summit of Mount Mitchell, but the Mountain Retreat Association declined to give them a figure of the cost for the proposed right-of-way.

The September 24, 1921, edition of the *Asheville Citizen* recorded that "both sides were heard in an argument on the proposed scenic motor road." Spokespersons for the Mount Mitchell Development Co. said that it had been charged that this road would necessarily contaminate the water supply of Montreat. "Such a statement," the company held, "seems to us is very far-fetched and totally disregards the real facts in the matter. We do not see how the road passing over the watershed, if such be true of the Montreat road, will in any way or manner injure Montreat. Undoubtedly there are roads and railroads in great numbers running over the watersheds of practically every town and city in North Carolina, except Asheville and possibly Old Fort and a few other towns situated in the mountains, and those watersheds are not contaminated."

Dr. R.C. Anderson retorted that the "proposed automobile road to be built by the Mount Mitchell Development Co. strikes a death blow at these two vital points: First the pollution of the water supply; second, the splitting of the Montreat grounds nearly half in two with a belt sixty feet wide and six miles long, exposing the institution to the irresponsible public."

On October 10, 1921, Judge Walter Brock issued a restraining order against Mount Mitchell Development Company which prohibited them from starting the proposed turnpike through Montreat, by way of the old railroad route. The Mountain Retreat Association claimed that the highway would damage the watershed near Black Mountain, and the Development Company was ordered to appear before the court on October 20, 1921, to show cause why the company should not be permanently enjoined from building the highway.

Then on October 21, 1921, the hearing on the injunction began in Superior court. Judge Thomas A. Jones opened the dispute, and the hearing continued on October 22. Judge Jones argued that "the association then had properties valued at a million dollars, and to permit the development company to build a road over its lands would injure their watershed, which they claimed, was one of the chief attractions of the assembly grounds." He further pointed out that the association had developed the grounds for twenty years, but the development company had not invested in large proportions. On December 10, 1921, the case was completed, and a final decision on the case would be handed down from the State Supreme Court in a few months.

Making Mount Mitchell accessible was the task that was in full swing in January of 1922. About a mile had already been paved in cinders, and rapid progress was being made upon the downward descent. The Mount Mitchell Development Company, it was learned, was pushing the construction of the scenic highway destined to become of paramount value not only to Western North Carolina, but also to all of the east, "where teeming millions turn their eyes in vacation time to a playground of superlatives."

The headlines of April 9, 1922, read, "**WILL CHANGE ROAD TO MOUNT MITCHELL**." The company had until March 31, 1923, to make the change so as not to cross the watershed. The Mount Mitchell Development Co. intended to grade the road to the summit of Mount Mitchell before March 1, 1923, to avoid crossing the lands and watershed of the Mountain Retreat Association, Presbyterian assembly grounds, according to R.C. Anderson, president of the association. During the last week of May 1922, work on the Mount Mitchell Motor Road was pressing on. The work force was large, and the grading crew had come to Toe River Gap, while the resurfacing crew was at Pinnacle.

The cinder surfacing of the road had stood the test from the heavy rains, leaving the road builders enthusiastic. The new toll road was made with grades of three to six percent.

The first automobiles were rolling up the road just one year after logging ceased and only three years after the passenger railroad had been discontinued. The Mount Mitchell Motor Road was dedicated on June 26, 1922. Special guests were invited, railroad brass was asked in, and there were hundreds of news reporters. All were there to make that special first trip to Camp Alice.

The Mount Mitchell Railroad and the Mount Mitchell Motor Road were very much alike. Both routed on or near the same roadbed. Fred A. Perley took charge of the motor road by being the president of the Mount Mitchell Development Co., which operated the toll road. Furthermore, one of the orginal partners of the Dickey, Campbell and Co.— C.A. Dickey—came to serve as the toll road's secretary. Finally, the traffic and promotion manager was none other that Sandford H. Cohen, who had been the General Passenger Agent for the Mount Mitchell railroad. One of Cohen's best known phrases to back the motor road was, "Making the apex of Appalachia accessible."

At about the same time that the Mount Mitchell Toll Road was being used, Ewart Wilson, the grandson of Big Tom Wilson, was determined to construct a motor toll road over one of the old logging railroad grades on the Yancey County side of the Black Mountains. Using local residents of Yancey County for labor, he completed the toll road in 1925, and it was dedicated and named the Big Tom Wilson Motor Road, commemorating a well-known resident of the upper Cane River valley. The route of the road began just south of Pensacola and continued toward Stepps Gap for a total distance of about 11 miles. From Stepps Gap, the road continued on the ridgeline for two miles, coming within a quarter-mile of the summit of Mount Mitchell. (It followed part of the present State Highway 128.) Since both of the toll roads connected at Stepps Gap, tourists could make a loop trip across the Black Mountains and tour the towns of Asheville, Black Mountain, Burnsville, and Mars Hill. The grade of the Big Tom Wilson Motor Road was steeper than that of the Mount Mitchell Toll Road, about 7½ percent, and was more rugged than the Mount Mitchell Toll Road. These poorer conditions caused the Big Tom Wilson Motor Road to receive much less traffic than the toll road in Buncombe County.

Warden Simmons, who was the gatekeeper and caretaker of Camp Alice, stated that a few of the most often asked questions by tourists were:

"How far is it to the top from here?"

"How come the mountain is so bare?"

"Why can't we go down now?"

"Why is the spring water so cold?"

"Are there any snakes here?"

Benches were placed about every 300 yards on the trail to provide a resting place for the weary. The average hiker could make the trip in thirty minutes without rushing, while coming down was much faster.

Because the road was wide enough only for one-way traffic, special regulations were required. Automobiles were allowed to begin their ascent only between the hours of 8:00 a.m. and 1:00 p.m., and they were required to start down the mountain between 3:30 p.m. and 5:30 p.m. Persons remaining on the mountain overnight were obliged to plan their descents so that they would arrive at the lower end of the road prior to 7:30 a.m. The cost of the trip was $1.00 per adult and 50 cents for children between the ages of five and twelve, with no charge for children under five.

The trip to Camp Alice could now be made in a simple two-hour trip, which meant the 35 miles could be traveled in half the time possible with the railroad which preceeded it. But there was an ugly regulation reflecting the limited social outlooks of yesteryear: "no colored person [was] to be admitted over the road except those going as drivers, nurses, or attendants, accompanied by employers."

The speed limit on the road was fifteen miles per hour.

Finley Stepp left the gatehouse after all of the cars had ascended or descended the toll road. He checked to see that the road was clear, and then assisted anyone that may have broken down on the trip up or down. He carried tools with him so he could change flat tires or make other minor repairs to get the cars back on their journey, so the road would remain clear.

In late September 1928, Cannonball Baker, a famed auto racer, set a world record, flashing up the course to Camp Alice in 35 minutes, 35 seconds. This was 5 minutes and 25 seconds faster than his previous record. Asheville received considerable publicity from this event.

W.B. Ferguson, District Engineer of the State Highway and Public Works Commission, wrote to Mr. Perley on November 21, 1935, advising him that the Highway Commission would not enter into an agreement for use of the road as discussed between Mr. Dickey, Mr. Ferguson, and Mr. Perley the week before. On December 2, 1935, a letter was written from J.Q. Gilkey to Mr. Albert Bauman, Montreat, N.C. The Chief Engineer of the Highway Department had come by Gilkey's home to discuss the Mount Mitchell Motor Road. Gilkey pointed out to him that the State should own the property. Bauman agreed with Gilkey and said he would like to see the State have it. He got the engineer to go over the property with him and place a value on it. Gilkey told Bauman that his part in the business transaction must be kept strictly confidential, as his position was one of an advisory capacity.

On March 10, 1936, Fred Perley wrote to Mr. Waynick, the Chairman of the State Highway Commission. There had been a conference two weeks before in Marion. They discussed the sale to the State of the motor road to Mount Mitchell. Mr. Dickey was in Florida at the time, so he was unable to give his views at the meeting. Knowing that the Federal Government was building the Blue Ridge Parkway, a free road, Dickey and Perley were eager to dispose of their property. Mr. Perley was advised that the State had agreed to furnish a toll-free road to Mount Mitchell State Park. Perley was hopeful that the Highway Commission would want his road by way of Black Mountain, and he hoped to sell it at a price to compensate for part of his investment.

On March 25, 1936, Fred Perley received a letter from J.S. Holmes, informing Mr. Perley that General McCloskey of Fort Bragg, N.C., would have a camp that summer to continue the development of the Mount Mitchell State Park.

On March 31, 1936, Mr. Perley replied to the foregoing letter while he was staying in Sanibel, Florida. Perley had made a trip to Black Mountain and met with Mr. Waynick and his committee in Marion, N.C., on February 25. Perley was hoping to get the state to take over his road, the Mount Mitchell Motor Road. On Perley's way back to Sanibel, he wrote Mr. Waynick again. He never received a reply, which he thought was quite strange. Perley read in the *Asheville Citizen* that Waynick had arranged for a toll-free road, which the Park Service wanted, but it was the Wilson road. Perley took it for granted that the Park Service would take the route to Mount Mitchell via Wilson road.

He asked Mr. Holmes to check up on the matter and write him back again.

The president of the Big Tom Wilson Motor Road and the Mount Mitchell Toll Road, Inc., A.E. Wilson, wrote to the State Highway and Public Works Commission in Raleigh, N.C., on April 3, 1936. He explained the agreement between the two parties on use of the toll road. It was agreed that the State's engineers and surveying crews could use the road, the CCC Camp of the U.S. and the U.S. Park Service could use it and for their contractors working on the Blue Ridge Parkway for transporting equipment, machinery, and supplies in Balsam Gap and other points on the Parkway that were convenient. The road had to be left in good condition and repair. The rivers and streams could not be polluted. The right was reserved to terminate the agreement if the Park Service opened a toll-free road to the summit of Mount Mitchell.

On April 14, 1936, a letter was written to Fred Perley from J.S. Holmes, State Forester, State of North Carolina Department of Conservation and Development, stating that the State Highway Commission had made an agreement with Big Tom Wilson to use their toll road for state and federal use connected with Mount Mitchell State Park and Scenic Highway. This was regarded as merely an arrangement made with the Division of Forestry. Those within the Department, however, felt the Mount Mitchell Road was of more use to them, and they wanted to come to a permanent understanding with Mr. Perley on a basis of assistance and maintenance of the road.

On April 18, 1936, J.S. Holmes, State Forester of the State of North Carolina Department of Conservation and Development, wrote to C.A. Dickey. The Army and National Park Service had planned to use the road for conveyance to the park site. As soon as the weather cleared, the Army officers planned to make the trip up for a reconnaissance so that work could commence on the construction of the park. The letter requested the U.S. Army have access to Mount Mitchell to inspect Camp Alice at 8:30 a.m. on Wednesday, April 22, 1936.

On April 28, 1936, Mr. Perley replied to a letter of April 25 from Charles Ross, Esquire, General Counsel, State Highway and Public Works Commission, Raleigh, N.C. Enclosed was a copy of the agreement made between the Commission and the Big Tom Wilson, Mount Mitchell Toll Road. He suggested a similar agreement for the Mount Mitchell Motor Road. J.C. Holmes, the Army, and Park Service had been there the week before. They were anxious to get the agreement, and Perley was most willing to cooperate. Mr. Perley requested to have a personal conference between Mr. Ross, himself, and Mr. Dickey.

On April 29, 1936, J.S. Holmes requested permission of Mr. Perley for Thomas W. Morse, Holmes's assistant in charge of State Parks, and three other men with the CCC program to go up to Mount Mitchell the next Monday morning and spend until Wednesday with Ed Wilson to look over all features of the CCC's proposed work.

On May 26, 1937, the State Highway and Public Works Commission billed Fred Perley for payment of his share ($100 per month) of maintenance on the Mount Mitchell Motor Road.

On April 1, 1938, Mr. Holmes wrote to Mr. Dickey requesting that the State Highway and Public Works Commission renew the agreement for use of the toll road for CCC camp purposes. Mr. Holmes thought the National Park Service was planning to move the camp in early May.

On April 5, 1938, Mr. Ferguson wrote to Mr. Dickey, stating that, weather permitting, on Monday, April 11, 1938, R.E. Morgan planned to start the section of the toll road from Toe River Gap to Wilson's Camp. A crew of prisoners would be at the toll gate at 8:00 a.m. on that date. It was arranged to let them in each day until work was finished.

Cover from Mount Mitchell brochure, which was given to tourists who visited Mount Mitchell by way of the motor toll road. Note that the "p" dips down to shown the location of Mount Mitchell.

The Demise of the Motor Toll Road

When work began on the Blue Ridge Parkway in 1935, the future of the Mount Mitchell Motor Road and the Big Tom Wilson Motor Road was uncertain. Then in 1939, the work crews had finished the portion of the Parkway between N.C. Highway 80 and Black Mountain Gap, leaving the toll roads in suspended animation.

The toll roads could have remained functional for a while; however, the people of North Carolina yearned for every state road to become toll-free. Therefore in 1940, six and a half miles of the toll road from the Blue Ridge Parkway Dead End at Black Mountain Gap was widened and enhanced from there to the end of the old Big Tom Wilson Motor Road near the summit of Mount Mitchell. This was the first motor road to Mount Mitchell that visitors could tour toll-free. Since the Blue Ridge Parkway construction was nearly completed, and the toll-free motor road was under way, the remainder of the motor roads on the Big Tom Wilson Motor Road and the Mount Mitchell Motor Road became superfluous and economically impractical, so they quickly came to a standstill.

The three wooden trestles that once stood on the Mount Mitchell Railroad have disappeared, rotted away. Even in 1960, very few crossties remained, and only an occasional spike can now be found. Because of the undergrowth, many areas were almost impassable, making the railroad bed difficult to follow, hard to detect.

The old stone tower on Mount Mitchell was erected and endowed to the state of North Carolina by Charles J. Harris of Dillsboro. The stone used in its construction was quarried from Mount Mitchell. It took two years to complete and was finished by 1926. It was built so that the wardens could keep a sharp lookout for fires. That tower was torn down on June 4, 1959.

In 1982 there was a renewed interest in the reopening of the narrow gauge railroad to the top of Mount Mitchell. The Economic Development Committee of the Black Mountain Chamber of Commerce studied the commercial and environmental effects of reopening the old toll road from Black Mountain to Mount Mitchell as a railroad.

The following five paragraphs contain information extracted from an unpublished report prepared that year by the TVA.

Local town and Buncombe County officials met with the Black Mountain Chamber of Commerce, along with the Carolina Sea-Sky Association, in 1966 to petition the Hon. Joseph M. Hunt Jr., then a state highway commissioner, to request that a new road be constructed from U.S. 70 east from Montreat Road to the Old Toll Road. They also petitioned for a new road to be built north from U.S. 70 from the Old Toll Road for six and a half miles to Black Mountain gap, where it would join the Blue Ridge Parkway. The Sea-Sky Road extension would pass under the Parkway and connect with N.C. 128, which leads to Mount Mitchell State Park, and would have crossed through Montreat Assembly property.

Five years before this petition, a traffic-counting survey was made to see how many visitors passed through the intersection of N.C. 128 and the Parkway; the total was more than 830,000. It was thought that many park visitors would look for a nearby town to find sleeping accommodations and that a more direct access was needed. Officials of the Swannanoa-Black Mountain Chamber of Commerce met with state officials in January 1982 to look at the three possibilities that the roadway could take.

Unfortunately, the plans to build such a road failed and were abandoned because of economic factors. At that time, some of the Buncombe and McDowell county residents felt that inaccessibility was desired. Residents were concerned that this much development might cause the Black Mountain area to be over-commercialized. However, from that public meeting, the idea of building a narrow gauge railroad to Mount Mitchell was suggested. It would have provided year-round access.

Members of the EDC met with Allan Paul, who was supervising the restoration of the Climax locomotive now on display at the Cradle of Forestry Museum near Brevard. After viewing Paul's slide presentation of the restoration of the Climax, then under way in the Tweetsie Railroad shop, the question was raised as to the purchase of new railroad equipment instead of the restoration of older equipment. For the older engines, many parts are no longer available, and replacement parts must be handcrafted, which is cost prohibitive.

Paul discussed what would be required to construct a safe track over the existing roadbed. This covered the proper weight of rail, type of treated timbers, ballast, and so on, which would be needed to accomplish that goal. His estimated construction cost of the track was at $30 a foot. It would have been a long-term project, more than five years to complete the work. Funding for the project was to come from within and outside the area from different investors. Concerning who would regulate construction and operation of the railroad (and important questions on the environment), the Chamber was to approach local state legislators to sponsor a bill that would enact the establishment of a Citizens Railroad Commission of five to seven members, to be appointed by the governor upon recommendations put forward by the Chamber. Raising the necessary capital and obtaining the needed right-of-ways were not seen as serious problems.

Despite the note of optimism in this report, the railroad line did not materialize because funding prospects proved too remote. And, as in the old days, Montreat was opposed to having the railroad north of their watershed; it was as if Mr. Perley and Mr. Crockett had returned. And Ridgecrest didn't want it near their watershed. Furthermore, the Park Service gave depressing news of the enormous task it would be to build a tunnel under the Blue Ridge Parkway.

The plan died.

Reflections

Author's Field Trip, August 1990

On this expedition I hoped to make on-site inspections of the route of the roadbed to and from Camp Alice and to recheck the USGS figures for the elevation of Camp Alice. The distance to Camp Alice from the Mount Mitchell State Park Road is 3.8 miles one-way. Although it is much easier and faster to walk to Camp Alice from Stepps Gap, I had not traveled this portion of the road yet, so I started from Highway #128. At a leisurely pace it takes about three hours to reach Camp Alice from the state road.

I did not know what I might see or find; but I didn't have to walk very far before I discovered something I had never dreamed would still exist: CROSSTIES. Most of them were waterlogged from the runoff of water that comes down from Mount Mitchell and the surrounding mountains. I was even more flabbergasted when I saw that many of the ties retained their original width and length. I counted close to 50 ties over the entire length of the roadbed. These remaining crossties had survived over 75 years! This discovery made the trip even more exciting.

The breathtaking views were an added bonus. I also spotted the remains of two small trestles that had fallen into the brooks that they once spanned. Sometimes I could even see the abutments, which were made of field rocks stacked on top of each other in small walls, which supported the timbers of the trestles. I expanded my search in and around these areas and found a beam nail that was over eight inches in length.

There were different lengths of spikes used on the Mount Mitchell Railroad. On this climb, I found only the shortest size of the three. I found four spikes on this trip, and the one that I recovered from Camp Alice was broken.

Author's Field Trip, September 30, 1990

This trip came very close to being disastrous. My partner and I started from Lookout Road Trail, which leads from the parking lot on Lookout Road in Montreat. The trail takes you just beyond the Rainbow Gap area of the roadbed. We traveled the roadbed from there to Long Gap, where we made a left turn. It was a part of the railroad bed we had followed two years earlier. I soon remembered that we had been there once before, but we failed to see more than about a mile of the road past Long Gap.

I had found only two spikes when we began having difficulty staying on this seldom-used section of the roadbed. This must have been one of the no-man's-land portions of the road that my old friend Sam Foreman had told me about. He said that certain parts of the roadbed were overgrown and travel would be difficult. Rocks had fallen into the road; trees also had fallen over the roadbed. Obviously, this meant that certain parts of the road would be less discernible than others. The trail was becoming more and more dense, until we were pushing tree limbs out of our faces and climbing over trees each step of the way.

We entered an area that looked like Slaty Cliffs, and it must have been somewhere near Pot Cove Gap. We noticed a rock below us that appeared to span 100 feet wide and 100 feet down. It was almost straight down, so anyone that had the misfortune of stepping off the roadbed would probably not survive the fall. This was about 12:30 to 1:00 p.m.

We were accompanied by a Border collie that led the way. I was in the middle, and my partner brought up the rear. After the dog and I had passed a certain point there, my partner passed the same spot and noticed something out of the corner of her eye. She called my attention to the fact that we had just passed by a snake, and although she had never seen one, she thought it had been a rattlesnake.

I turned to look back, and I became aware of the awful sight before me. It was a three-and-a-half-foot yellow phase timber rattler. It had placed itself beside the path we had just passed through. My first reaction was fear, and all I could do was stare into its evil yellow eyes. I told my partner to find the biggest stick she could, and after a minute or so, she replied to me that she could not find any. I repeated my plea to her, with a bit more urgency, because the reptile was beginning to make a methodical approach toward me.

She returned with a limb that she had found, and I cautiously poised it in a strike position, just above its massive head. I took my first swing and broke the decayed limb in two different places. It was at that moment that the snake began to shake its rattle profusely in a defensive posture. It was only a moment earlier that I had been transfixed looking into its vicious eyes. Meanwhile, it was advancing toward me using its forked tongue to get my position. And it was only a few short minutes before that since the three of us had brushed right by it.

With nowhere to go, except up a sheer rock face or down a steep cliff off of the road, I frantically realized that the use of the limb was futile, and without taking my eyes off of the snake, I quickly told my partner to hand me another weapon as soon as possible. She promptly responded by handing me a large rock.

I hurled the rock with all of my force, and the snake's neck was broken by a severe crushing blow. I told my partner to drop the rocks, and I knelt down. Using a sharp pocketknife, I beheaded the serpent in one quick cut.

Some folks would rather be bitten than to kill a poisonous snake, but I am not one of them. It matters not to me whether the snake is in a populated area or not. If it's a threatening situation, the snake "gets it" in my book, every time.

We decided that, since more snake encounters would be likely and we were four or five miles away from help, we would call off our trip for the day. I slid the carcass into my sack and we cautiously headed back to the car. Ironically, I was probably closer to finding the spot where the alleged lost engine was than I had ever been before. I was also closer to being bitten by a seven-year-old rattlesnake than I had ever been before. I hope that the next timber rattler I see is in a glass enclosure at the Nature Center.

We will continue our trips after all of the leaves have fallen and the weather is not warm enough to attract rattlers to bask in the midday sun near their den. Incidentally, I wear its hide today as a good luck charm on one of my belts.

Afterword

There have been many stories told of the alleged locomotives that toppled off the grade into the valley. Many old-timers said that there was an engine near the Montreat boundary; others said that there was one closer to Graybeard Mountain.

A few years ago, a group of firemen reported to have stumbled over an engine while conducting maneuvers. It was said to have been upside down, with only one-half of the wheels exposed. Ironically, none of the men ever found the wreck again, even after extensive searches in and around that area.

Many people still believe that in some remote place in those mountains lies an iron horse, although most have concluded it to be nothing more than an old wives' tale. After making extensive searches from Montreat to Pot Cove Gap, I found no locomotive. My personal belief is that the firemen may have seen a part of a loader, or possibly even part of a skidder, and if there is something like that still in existence up there, it would be in very poor condition. As time goes by, I will continue my search, as many have done before me, for this ghost train which is supposed to be lost in history.

There's an open-cut near Black Mountain, on the old railroad bed, that has remained very much the same as it was 75 years ago. Whenever I walk through that cut, I feel as though a locomotive is barreling towards me. It's hard to explain this strange sensation, and it has happened to me on more than one occasion, in that very same place.

But the experience I had walking the old railroad bed at night, during late summer in 1990, was even more mysterious. At night, the area around Long Gap seems to transform to a gloomy, somewhat frightening place. I traveled on foot for several miles on the old roadbed, but this particular area around Long Gap was the only spot that I felt disquieted.

It was a warm late summer night as I passed through Long Gap. Only a few short minutes after I had passed the old bear hunters' cabin on the side of the road, fog suddenly rolled up the mountainside over the edge of the ridge. It was an eerie feeling to see the fog come in so quickly, swelling back and forth up the ridge around me. And it was chilling to see the fog from the light that was cast through the lantern I was carrying. At that very same moment, my lantern stopped burning, and the distant moon, glowing through the fog, made my blood run cold. I managed to relight the lantern, and I moved away from the area in a panic-stricken trot. When I got close to Montreat, the terror that I had encountered passed.

Since that time, I have not made another visit to Long Gap at night, nor can I explain the occurrence that took place that night. It was too inexplainably strange to make sense of. Perhaps something terrible happened there on the Mount Mitchell line, so many years ago.

There are many ways to walk the old roadbed, if you want to see the beauty of the mountains. If you wish to travel the upper reaches of the line, then the Blue Ridge Parkway would be your best route. You must first register your vehicle with the ranger station and choose a safe place to park. If the lower limits are of more interest to you, then you can enter the road at several points in Montreat. They have several different trail maps there to use when you go. You can also walk the old railroad bed by parking near the new roadside historical marker that I lobbied so long for near the Old Toll Road junction at Old US 70 Highway. If you choose to go this route, you must be familiar with the switchbacks, or you will wander off the road into private lands. Remember to take a partner with you.

The once-in-a-lifetime experience of riding the rails to Mount Mitchell will probably never happen again, but this paramount piece of Western North Carolina history will never be forgotten.

Photo
Album

View of the route of the railroad passing through the Montreat Assembly grounds. (Dept. of History, Montreat)

Momentary stop on the railroad line headed down the grade loaded with logs. (Biddix)

Engine shrouded in steam while making its way down the mountain slopes with another load of logs. (Biddix)

Logging train loaded with logs makes brief stop at one of the curves on the Mount Mitchell Railroad. The fireman, engineer, and brakeman pose for this photograph. (Biddix)

Workers take a short break at their outdoor restroom (outhouse) facilities.

A view from the track level of one of the work engines on the Mount Mitchell Railroad. Note the tool box and oil drums on the front of the engine. (Biddix/Gregg)

Photo of several loads of logs in the mill pond at the sawmill. These logs were waiting to be pulled into the mill to be ripped into lumber. Note the dry-packed finished lumber in the background. (Casstevens)

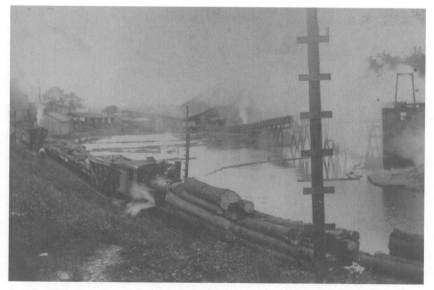

Load of logs heading into the sawmill that was located just east of the town of Black Mountain. Part of the engine shop can be seen in the background at the left of the photo. (Biddix)

Photo showing steep curve on the Mount Mitchell Railroad at Slaty Mountain, taken between 1915 and 1919. (Barnhill)

Another sharp curve on the Mount Mitchell Railroad. (Barnhill)

Photo with view of the Mount Mitchell train ascending Big Slaty Mountain. The train is barely visible, by a puff of smoke in the upper center of the picture. The view is from Long Gap on the Mount Mitchell railroad. (Barnhill)

The Mount Mitchell Railroad on Slaty Mountain. (Barnhill)

View of Pinnacle, 5693 ft. (Norfolk-Southern Archives)

View of Mount Mitchell from Toe River Gap. Mount Mitchell can be seen in the upper right. (Norfolk-Southern Archives)

Camp Alice in its early days. Shown here are flagstaff and tents for overnight accommodations. (Norfolk-Southern Archives)

Another view of Camp Alice. Rustic dining hall shown on the left, and two parked passenger coaches shown just below the loading and unloading platform. Outdoor bathroom facilities can also be seen to the right in the background. (Barnhill)

Passengers board the train to leave Camp Alice. (Norfolk-Southern Archives)

Camp Alice in the 1930s. It had the distinction of being the largest overnight accommodations in the Black Mountains. (Dept. of History, Montreat)

Camp Alice, the end of the scenic tourist railroad line. (Norfolk-Southern Archives)

Mrs. Fred Perley prepares for a photo while sitting in front of a friend on a track car, sometimes called velocipede. (Casstevens)

Author's shot of present-day Camp Alice.

Another angle of present-day Camp Alice.

Empty train sits on a section of track at Commissary Ridge. Note one of the workers standing on crutches. Accidents were very common due to the dangerous nature of the work, such as primitive link and pin couplers. (Biddix)

Dual gauge trestle that stood near the present I-40 near Black Mountain. While making some repairs, section crew poses for the cameraman. (Biddix)

Pictured in front of a Mount Mitchell Shay locomotive are engineer "Big Jim" Oliver Burgin on the left, and his fireman, Vernon Elliot, on the right. They seem to be dressed up for the occasion. (Burgin)

Giant steam skidder belches smoke while workers show off their next load ready for hauling. (Biddix)

Photo shows destruction of the Elisha Mitchell Monument. (American Forestry)

Mount Mitchell from Mt. Hallback. Note dead trees, even in 1916. Also note the observation tower built by Perley and Crockett. It can be seen on the summit, in the upper left. (Norfolk-Southern Archives)

Trainload of logs pulled by a Climax locomotive pauses near the top, before coming down the slopes of the mountains. (Casstevens)

Photo of the destruction of part of Mount Mitchell, after a fire that followed the lumbermen. (American Forestry)

Climax engine No. 8 and another unidentified Climax work at a log loading site near the slopes of Mount Mitchell. Climax No. 8 was purchased new in 1914. (Biddix)

Climax engine No. 4 pauses on the way up the mountains with a large number of passengers. Note that the spark arrester is not in use. (Barnhill)

Passengers boarding the crude homemade coaches on a platform near the mill, at the Mount Mitchell Railroad Station. (Dept. of History, Montreat)

Early crude passenger cars at the Mount Mitchell Station. Also the Flag Station can be seen at the left of the train. The flag at the Flag Station went up when standard gauge trains moved on or off of the interchange from Southern Railway. (Burgin)

Bullhead Mountain and Craggy Dome in the distance. (Norfolk-Southern Archives)

View from the Slaty Mountains. (Barnhill)

A view of the railroad near Clingmans Peak. (Barnhill)

A view of a six-car passenger train at one of the switchbacks on the scenic railroad line. (Barnhill)

Cloudy day on the railroad. (Barnhill)

Standing at the rear of the train, pictured left to right: Misses Nannie Campbell, Annie Pemberton, Jean Pemberton, Mr. Castle, Misses Mary Hughes, Marie Pemberton, Helen Slocomb (later Mrs. F.A. Perley), and Mr. F.A. Perley. Seated is Mr. James Many. (Casstevens)

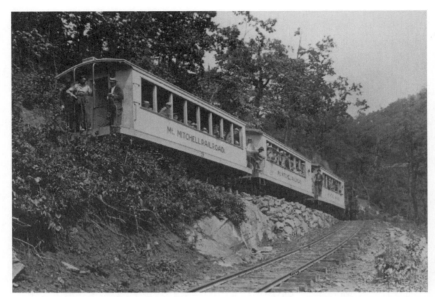

Climax locomotive pushes away from the second switchback, while the crowd of sightseers gazes at the photographer, William Barnhill. (Barnhill)

Trains seen here make use of a passing track, or siding, on Perley and Crockett's Mount Mitchell Railroad. Note crew standing on back of primitive work car as smoke comes from the chimney inside the car. (Casstevens)

Angry Climax brings passengers through Sourwood Gap. (Hemphill)

Passenger train on the way to Camp Alice. Mitchell Ridge is in the background. Photo was taken on September 4, 1917, by McCanlest.

Climax engine pulling passenger train to Mount Mitchell. (Dept. of History, Montreat)

Scenic train at Graybeard Mountain. Note primitive water tower at the right of the train. (Norfolk-Southern Archives)

Perley and Crockett Climax No. 3 sits on dual gauge trackage at the company's engine house near Black Mountain. Two other Climax engines can be seen behind this engine. Note one of the crude passenger coaches behind Climax No. 3. Apparently, these cars were built to Perley and Crockett's specifications at the Southern Railways shop. (Biddix)

View of Pinnacle in the background with the Mount Mitchell Railroad in the foreground. (Barnhill)

View of the Mount Mitchell motor road near Pinnacle. (Dept. of History, Montreat)

The gate at the beginning of the toll road near Black Mountain. (Casstevens)

Dickey and Campbell Engine No. 6 couples with two boxcars of finished lumber at the company mill near Black Mountain. The 0-4-0 was built by the Cooke Locomotive and Machine Co. of Paterson, New Jesery. Dickey and Campbell purchased the secondhand engine from the Southern Iron and Equipment Co., dealers in used locomotives, in 1913.

Dickey and Campbell Loader No. 1 grabs a log for the log cars. This loader is by the American Log Loader Company.

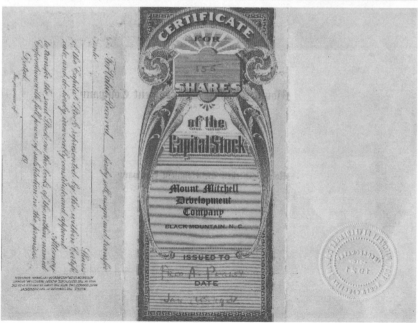

Mount Mitchell development company stock certificate. (Casstevens)

Bibliography

1. *American Forestry.* Vol. XXI, February 1915, pp. 88. 89.
2. *Asheville Citizen.* November 24, 1910; November 2, 1911; March 29, 1912; June 21, 1912; June 1, 1913; July 23, 1913; August 24, 1913; October 8, 1913; June 9, 1914; June 22, 1914; July 8, 1914; August 19, 1914; January 4, 1915; January 13, 1915; February 23, 1915; April 1, 1915; May 20, 1915; July 2, 1915; July 15, 1915; July 18, 1915; August 1, 1915; August 9, 1915; September 12, 1915; September 24, 1915; November 14, 1915; November 20, 1915; December 16, 1915; January 14, 1916; April 5, 1916; May 28, 1916; June 13, 1916; July 21, 1916; October 3, 1916; July 31, 1917; November 11, 1917; July 22, 1918; August 4, 1918; August 25, 1918; September 26, 1918; October 3, 1918; July 6, 1921; August 9, 1921; August 28, 1921; September 1, 1921; September 16, 1921; September 24, 1921; October 11, 1921; October 22, 1921; December 11, 1921; January 1, 1922; April 9, 1922; July 14, 1929; June 4, 1959.
3. Anderson, Reverend Robert Campbell, **The Story of Montreat from its Beginning: 1897-1947,** pp. 36, 37.
4. Biddix, Willard James. Black Mountain, N.C. Interview on August 3, 1990. The late Mr. Biddix was the son of one of the overhead skidder operators.
5. Burgin, Reverend Gorman. Black Mountain, N.C. Phone conversation March 18, 1988. He is the only surviving son of Engineer (Big Jim Oliver Burgin).
6. Casler, Walter. Corry, Penna. Several letters from October 1990 to August 1991.
7. *Charlotte Observer.* July 1915.
8. Crockett, Robert P. Williamsport, Penna. Several letters from July 1990 to September 1991.
9. Foreman, Samuel L. "Lumbering in Montreat." September 1967. pp. 6, 11, 19.
10. *Historical Foundation News.* Presbyterian Church (U.S.A.) Department of History, Montreat, N.C.
11. "History of Black Mountain, North Carolina." By the senior class of 1933 at the Black Mountain High School, p. 24.
12. Kerlee, Carl. Black Mountain, N.C. Phone conversation.
13. Koch, Michael. **Steam and Thunder in the Timber.** 1979, pp. 41, 45, 50.

14. Lane, Mary. Presbyterian Historical Foundation of the Presbyterian and Reformed Churches. Conversation September 1988.
15. *Mountain Living Magazine.* May 1982, pp. 5, 6 and June 1982, pp. 8, 9.
16. Padgett, Mac. Black Mountain, N.C. Phone conversation. December, 1990.
17. Paul, Allan. Raleigh, N.C. Letters from October 1990 to February 1992.
18. **Deed Book, Buncombe County.** Reference #DB 161/434, 161/554, 182/245, 182/321, 186/59, 186/225, 206/67.
19. Schwarzkopf, Kent. **A History of Mt. Mitchell and the Black Mountains.** 1985, pp. 82-108.
20. *Southern Lumberman.* August 2, 1913.
21. Tennessee Valley Authority. ''Preliminary Engineering report for the Proposed Black Mountain—Mt. Mitchell Passenger Railroad in North Carolina'' 1982.
22. Van Noppen, Ina and John. **Western North Carolina Since the Civil War.** 1973, pp. 373-377.